Harvard Business Review

ON

LEADERSHIP

THE HARVARD BUSINESS REVIEW PAPERBACK SERIES

The series is designed to bring today's managers and professionals the fundamental information they need to stay competitive in a fast-moving world. From the preeminent thinkers whose work has defined an entire field to the rising stars who will redefine the way we think about business, here are the leading minds and landmark ideas that have established the *Harvard Business Review* as required reading for ambitious businesspeople in organizations around the globe.

Other books in the series:

Harvard Business Review on Change

Harvard Business Review on Knowledge Management

Harvard Business Review on Measuring Corporate Performance

Harvard Business Review on Strategies for Growth

Harvard Business Review

ON

LEADERSHIP

A HARVARD BUSINESS REVIEW PAPERBACK

Contents

The Manager's Job: *Folklore and Fact*   1
HENRY MINTZBERG

What Leaders Really Do   37
JOHN P. KOTTER

Managers and Leaders: *Are They Different?*   61
ABRAHAM ZALEZNIK

The Discipline of Building Character   89
JOSEPH L. BADARACCO, JR.

The Ways Chief Executive Officers Lead   115
CHARLES M. FARKAS AND SUZY WETLAUFER

The Human Side of Management   147
THOMAS TEAL

The Work of Leadership   171
RONALD A. HEIFETZ AND DONALD L. LAURIE

Whatever Happened to the Take-Charge Manager?   199
NITIN NOHRIA AND JAMES D. BERKLEY

About the Contributors   223

Index   227

Harvard Business Review

ON
LEADERSHIP

The Manager's Job

Folklore and Fact

HENRY MINTZBERG

Executive Summary

HRB REGULARLY REPRINTS "CLASSIC" ARTICLES that are at least 15 years old and that have demonstrated enduring value.

In this issue, we present a thoughtful analysis of what the manager really does. Originally printed in the July–August 1975 issue, Henry Mintzberg's study continues to speak to readers' needs. Requests for reprints for the last two years alone total more than 22,000.

Henry Mintzberg asks, "What do managers do?" After conducting his own study of five CEOs and analyzing other studies of managers and how they work, he concludes that managerial work involves interpersonal roles, informational roles, and decisional roles. These roles require a number of skills: developing peer relationships, carrying out negotiations, motivating subordinates, resolving conflicts, establishing information networks and disseminating information, making decisions with little or ambiguous information, and allocating resources.

The author uses his own and other research to present a series of documented facts that debunk myths about managers and how they work. Finally, he argues that a good manager is an introspective manager and offers a series of questions designed to help managers analyze themselves and their jobs.

Mintzberg also contributes a commentary outlining his perspective 15 years later.

If you ask managers what they do, they will most likely tell you that they plan, organize, coordinate, and control. Then watch what they do. Don't be surprised if you can't relate what you see to these words.

When a manager is told that a factory has just burned down and then advises the caller to see whether temporary arrangements can be made to supply customers through a foreign subsidiary, is that manager planning, organizing, coordinating, or controlling? How about when he or she presents a gold watch to a retiring employee? Or attends a conference to meet people in the trade and returns with an interesting new product idea for employees to consider?

These four words, which have dominated management vocabulary since the French industrialist Henri Fayol first introduced them in 1916, tell us little about what managers actually do. At best, they indicate some vague objectives managers have when they work.

The field of management, so devoted to progress and change, has for more than half a century not seriously addressed *the* basic question: What do managers do? Without a proper answer, how can we teach management? How can we design planning or information systems for managers? How can we improve the practice of management at all?

Our ignorance of the nature of managerial work shows up in various ways in the modern organization—in boasts by successful managers who never spent a single day in a management training program; in the turnover of corporate planners who never quite understood what it was the manager wanted; in the computer consoles gathering dust in the back room because the managers never used the fancy on-line MIS some analyst thought they needed. Perhaps most important, our ignorance shows up in the inability of our large public organizations to come to grips with some of their most serious policy problems. (See "Retrospective Commentary" on page 29.)

What do managers do? Even managers themselves don't always know.

Somehow, in the rush to automate production, to use management science in the functional areas of marketing and finance, and to apply the skills of the behavioral scientist to the problem of worker motivation, the manager—the person in charge of the organization or one of its subunits—has been forgotten.

I intend to break the reader away from Fayol's words and introduce a more supportable and useful description of managerial work. This description derives from my review and synthesis of research on how various managers have spent their time.

In some studies, managers were observed intensively; in a number of others, they kept detailed diaries; in a few studies, their records were analyzed. All kinds of managers were studied—foremen, factory supervisors, staff managers, field sales managers, hospital administrators, presidents of companies and nations, and even street gang leaders. These "managers" worked in the United States, Canada, Sweden, and Great Britain. (See "Research on Managerial Work" on page 27.)

A synthesis of these findings paints an interesting picture, one as different from Fayol's classical view as a cubist abstract is from a Renaissance painting. In a sense, this picture will be obvious to anyone who has ever spent a day in a manager's office, either in front of the desk or behind it. Yet, at the same time, this picture throws into doubt much of the folklore that we have accepted about the manager's work.

Folklore and Facts About Managerial Work

There are four myths about the manager's job that do not bear up under careful scrutiny of the facts.

Folklore: The manager is a reflective, systematic planner. The evidence on this issue is overwhelming, but not a shred of it supports this statement.

Fact: Study after study has shown that managers work at an unrelenting pace, that their activities are characterized by brevity, variety, and discontinuity, and that they are strongly oriented to action and dislike reflective activities. Consider this evidence:

Half the activities engaged in by the five chief executives of my study lasted less than nine minutes, and only 10% exceeded one hour.[1] A study of 56 U.S. foremen found that they averaged 583 activities per eight-hour shift, an average of 1 every 48 seconds.[2] The work pace for both chief executives and foremen was unrelenting. The chief executives met a steady stream of callers and mail from the moment they arrived in the morning until they left in the evening. Coffee breaks and lunches were inevitably work related, and ever-present subordinates seemed to usurp any free moment.

A diary study of 160 British middle and top managers found that they worked without interruption for a half hour or more only about once every two days.[3]

Of the verbal contacts the chief executives in my study engaged in, 93% were arranged on an ad hoc basis. Only 1% of the executives' time was spent in open-ended observational tours. Only 1 out of 368 verbal contacts was unrelated to a specific issue and could therefore be called general planning. Another researcher found that "in *not one single case* did a manager report obtaining important external information from a general conversation or other undirected personal communication."[4]

How often can you work for a half hour without interruption?

Is this the planner that the classical view describes? Hardly. The manager is simply responding to the pressures of the job. I found that my chief executives terminated many of their own activities, often leaving meetings before the end, and interrupted their desk work to call in subordinates. One president not only placed his desk so that he could look down a long hallway but also left his door open when he was alone—an invitation for subordinates to come in and interrupt him.

Clearly, these managers wanted to encourage the flow of current information. But more significantly, they seemed to be conditioned by their own work loads. They appreciated the opportunity cost of their own time, and they were continually aware of their ever-present obligations—mail to be answered, callers to attend to, and so on. It seems that a manager is always plagued by the possibilities of what might be done and what must be done.

When managers must plan, they seem to do so implicitly in the context of daily actions, not in some abstract process reserved for two weeks in the organization's mountain retreat. The plans of the chief executives I studied seemed to exist only in their heads—as flexible, but often specific, intentions. The traditional literature notwithstanding, the job of managing does not breed reflective planners; managers respond to stimuli, they are conditioned by their jobs to prefer live to delayed action.

FOLKLORE: THE EFFECTIVE MANAGER HAS NO REGULAR DUTIES TO PERFORM. Managers are constantly being told to spend more time planning and delegating and less time seeing customers and engaging in negotiations. These are not, after all, the true tasks of the manager. To use the popular analogy, the good manager, like the good conductor, carefully orchestrates everything in advance, then sits back, responding occasionally to an unforeseeable exception. But here again the pleasant abstraction just does not seem to hold up.

Fact: Managerial work involves performing a number of regular duties, including ritual and ceremony, negotiations, and processing of soft information that links the organization with its environment. Consider some evidence from the research:

A study of the work of the presidents of small companies found that they engaged in routine activities because their companies could not afford staff specialists and were so thin on operating personnel that a single absence often required the president to substitute.[5]

One study of field sales managers and another of chief executives suggest that it is a natural part of both jobs to see important customers, assuming the managers wish to keep those customers.[6]

Someone, only half in jest, once described the manager as the person who sees visitors so that other people can get their work done. In my study, I found that certain ceremonial duties—meeting visiting dignitaries, giving out gold watches, presiding at Christmas dinners—were an intrinsic part of the chief executive's job.

Studies of managers' information flow suggest that managers play a key role in securing "soft" external information (much of it available only to them because of their status) and in passing it along to their subordinates.

FOLKLORE: THE SENIOR MANAGER NEEDS AGGRE-GATED INFORMATION, WHICH A FORMAL MANAGE-MENT INFORMATION SYSTEM BEST PROVIDES. Not too long ago, the words *total information system* were everywhere in the management literature. In keeping with the classical view of the manager as that individual perched on the apex of a regulated, hierarchical system, the literature's manager was to receive all important information from a giant, comprehensive MIS.

But lately, these giant MIS systems are not working—managers are simply not using them. The enthusiasm has waned. A look at how managers actually process information makes it clear why.

Fact: Managers strongly favor verbal media, telephone calls and meetings, over documents. Consider the following:

In two British studies, managers spent an average of 66% and 80% of their time in verbal (oral) communication.[7] In my study of five American chief executives, the figure was 78%.

These five chief executives treated mail processing as a burden to be dispensed with. One came in Saturday morning to process 142 pieces of mail in just over three hours, to "get rid of all the stuff." This same manager looked at the first piece of "hard" mail he had received all week, a standard cost report, and put it aside with the comment, "I never look at this."

Today's gossip may be tomorrow's fact— that's why managers cherish hearsay.

These same five chief executives responded immediately to 2 of the 40 routine reports they received during the five weeks of my study and to 4 items in the 104 periodicals. They skimmed most of these periodicals in seconds, almost ritualistically. In all, these chief executives of good-sized organizations initiated on their own—that is, not in response to something else—a grand total of 25 pieces of mail during the 25 days I observed them.

An analysis of the mail the executives received reveals an interesting picture—only 13% was of specific and immediate use. So now we have another piece in the puzzle: not much of the mail provides live, current information—the action of a competitor, the mood of a government legislator, or the rating of last night's television show. Yet this is the information that drove the managers, interrupting their meetings and rescheduling their workdays.

Consider another interesting finding. Managers seem to cherish "soft" information, especially gossip, hearsay, and speculation. Why? The reason is its timeliness; today's gossip may be tomorrow's fact. The manager who misses the telephone call revealing that the company's biggest customer was seen golfing with a main competitor may read about a dramatic drop in sales in the next quarterly report. But then it's too late.

To assess the value of historical, aggregated, "hard" MIS information, consider two of the manager's prime uses for information—to identify problems and opportunities[8] and to build mental models (e.g., how the organization's budget system works, how customers buy products, how changes in the economy affect the organization). The evidence suggests that the manager identifies decision situations and builds models not with the aggregated abstractions an MIS provides but with specific tidbits of data.

Consider the words of Richard Neustadt, who studied the information-collecting habits of Presidents Roosevelt, Truman, and Eisenhower: "It is not information of a general sort that helps a President see personal stakes; not summaries, not surveys, not the *bland amalgams*. Rather . . . it is the odds and ends of *tangible detail* that pieced together in his mind illuminate the underside of issues put before him. To help himself he must reach out as widely as he can for every scrap of fact, opinion, gossip, bearing on his interests and relationships as President. He must become his own director of his own central intelligence."[9]

The manager's emphasis on this verbal media raises two important points. First, verbal information is stored in the brains of people. Only when people write this information down can it be stored in the files of the organization—whether in metal cabinets or on magnetic tape—and managers apparently do not write down much of what they hear. Thus the strategic data bank of the organization is not in the memory of its computers but in the minds of its managers.

Second, managers' extensive use of verbal media helps to explain why they are reluctant to delegate tasks. It is not as if they can hand a dossier over to subordinates; they must take the time to "dump memory"—to tell subordinates all about the subject. But this could take so long that managers may find it easier to do the task themselves. Thus they are damned by their own information system to a "dilemma of delegation"—to do too much or to delegate to subordinates with inadequate briefing.

F OLKLORE: MANAGEMENT IS, OR AT LEAST IS QUICKLY BECOMING, A SCIENCE AND A PROFES-SION. By almost any definition of *science* and *profession*, this statement is false. Brief observation of any manager will quickly lay to rest the notion that managers practice a science. A science involves the enaction of systematic, analytically determined procedures or programs. If we do not even know what procedures managers use, how can we prescribe them by scientific analysis? And how can we call management a profession if we cannot specify what managers are to learn? For after all, a profession involves "knowledge of some department of learning or science" (*Random House Dictionary*).[10]

Fact: The managers' programs—to schedule time, process information, make decisions, and so on—remain locked deep inside their brains. Thus, to describe these programs, we rely on words like *judgment* and *intuition,* seldom stopping to realize that they are merely labels for our ignorance.

I was struck during my study by the fact that the executives I was observing—all very competent—are fundamentally indistinguishable from their counterparts of a hundred years ago (or a thousand years ago). The information they need differs, but they seek it in the same way—by word of mouth. Their decisions concern modern technology, but the procedures they use to make those decisions are the same as the procedures used by nineteenth century managers. Even the computer, so important for the specialized work of the organization, has apparently had no influence on the work procedures of general managers. In fact, the manager is in a kind of loop, with increasingly heavy work pressures but no aid forthcoming from management science.

Considering the facts about managerial work, we can see that the manager's job is enormously complicated and difficult. Managers are overburdened with obligations yet cannot easily delegate their tasks. As a result, they are driven to overwork and forced to do many tasks superficially. Brevity, fragmentation, and verbal communication characterize their work. Yet these are the very characteristics of managerial work that have impeded scientific attempts to improve it. As a result, management scientists have concentrated on the specialized functions of the organization, where it is easier to analyze the procedures and quantify the relevant information.[11]

But the pressures of a manager's job are becoming worse. Where before managers needed to respond only to owners and directors, now they find that subordinates with democratic norms continually reduce their freedom to issue unexplained orders, and a growing number of outside influences (consumer groups, government agencies, and so on) demand attention. Managers have had nowhere to turn for help. The first step in providing such help is to find out what the manager's job really is.

Back to a Basic Description of Managerial Work

Earlier, I defined the manager as that person in charge of an organization or subunit. Besides CEOs, this definition would include vice presidents, bishops, foremen, hockey coaches, and prime ministers. All these

The Manager's Roles

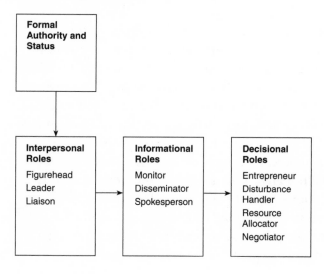

"managers" are vested with formal authority over an organizational unit. From formal authority comes status, which leads to various interpersonal relations, and from these comes access to information. Information, in turn, enables the manager to make decisions and strategies for the unit.

The manager's job can be described in terms of various "roles," or organized sets of behaviors identified with a position. My description, shown in "The Manager's Roles," comprises ten roles. As we shall see, formal authority gives rise to the three interpersonal roles, which in turn give rise to the three informational roles; these two sets of roles enable the manager to play the four decisional roles.

Interpersonal Roles

Three of the manager's roles arise directly from formal authority and involve basic interpersonal relationships. First is the *figurehead* role. As the head of an organizational unit, every manager must perform some ceremonial duties. The president greets the touring dignitaries. The foreman attends the wedding of a lathe operator. The sales manager takes an important customer to lunch.

The chief executives of my study spent 12% of their contact time on ceremonial duties; 17% of their incoming mail dealt with acknowledgments and requests related to their status. For example, a letter to a company president requested free merchandise for a crippled schoolchild; diplomas that needed to be signed were put on the desk of the school superintendent.

Duties that involve interpersonal roles may sometimes be routine, involving little serious communication and no important decision making. Nevertheless, they are important to the smooth functioning of an organization and cannot be ignored.

Managers are responsible for the work of the people of their unit. Their actions in this regard constitute the *leader* role. Some of these actions involve leadership directly—for example, in most organizations the managers are normally responsible for hiring and training their own staff.

In addition, there is the indirect exercise of the leader role. For example, every manager must motivate and encourage employees, somehow reconciling their individual needs with the goals of the organization. In virtually every contact with the manager, subordinates seeking leadership clues ask: "Does she approve?" "How would she like the report to turn out?" "Is she more interested in market share than high profits?"

The influence of managers is most clearly seen in the leader role. Formal authority vests them with great potential power; leadership determines in large part how much of it they will realize.

The literature of management has always recognized the leader role, particularly those aspects of it related to motivation. In comparison, until recently it has hardly mentioned the *liaison* role, in which the manager makes contacts outside the vertical chain of command. This is remarkable in light of the finding of virtually every study of managerial work that managers spend as much time with peers and other people outside their units as they do with their own subordinates—and, surprisingly, very little time with their own superiors.

In Rosemary Stewart's diary study, the 160 British middle and top managers spent 47% of their time with peers, 41% of their time with people inside their unit, and only 12% of their time with their superiors. For Robert H. Guest's study of U.S. foremen, the figures were 44%, 46%, and 10%. The chief executives of my study averaged 44% of their contact time with people outside their organizations, 48% with subordinates, and 7% with directors and trustees.

The contacts the five CEOs made were with an incredibly wide range of people: subordinates; clients, business associates, and suppliers; and peers—managers of similar organizations, government and trade organization officials, fellow directors on outside boards, and independents with no relevant organizational affiliations. The chief executives' time with and mail from these groups is shown in "The Chief Executive's Contacts." Guest's study of foremen shows, likewise, that their contacts were numerous and wide-ranging, seldom involving fewer than 25 individuals, and often more than 50.

The Chief Executive's Contacts

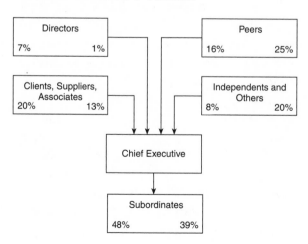

Informational Roles

By virtue of interpersonal contacts, both with subordinates and with a network of contacts, the manager
emerges as the nerve center of the organizational unit.
The manager may not know everything but typically
knows more than subordinates do.

Studies have shown this relationship to hold for all
managers, from street gang leaders to U.S. presidents. In
The Human Group, George C. Homans explains how,
because they were at the center of the information flow
in their own gangs and were also in close touch with
other gang leaders, street gang leaders were better
informed than any of their followers.[12] As for presidents,
Richard Neustadt observes: "The essence of {Franklin}
Roosevelt's technique for information-gathering was
competition. 'He would call you in,' one of his aides once
told me, 'and he'd ask you to get the story on some complicated business, and you'd come back after a couple of
days of hard labor and present the juicy morsel you'd
uncovered under a stone somewhere, and *then* you'd
find out he knew all about it, along with something else
you *didn't* know. Where he got this information from he
wouldn't mention, usually, but after he had done this to
you once or twice you got damn careful about *your*
information.'"[13]

We can see where Roosevelt "got this information"
when we consider the relationship between the interpersonal and informational roles. As leader, the manager
has formal and easy access to every staff member. In
addition, liaison contacts expose the manager to external information to which subordinates often lack access.
Many of these contacts are with other managers of equal
status, who are themselves nerve centers in their own

organization. In this way, the manager develops a powerful database of information.

Processing information is a key part of the manager's job. In my study, the CEOs spent 40% of their contact time on activities devoted exclusively to the transmission of information; 70% of their incoming mail was purely informational (as opposed to requests for action). Managers don't leave meetings or hang up the telephone to get back to work. In large part, communication *is* their work. Three roles describe these informational aspects of managerial work.

As *monitor*, the manager is perpetually scanning the environment for information, interrogating liaison contacts and subordinates, and receiving unsolicited information, much of it as a result of the network of personal contacts. Remember that a good part of the information the manager collects in the monitor role arrives in verbal form, often as gossip, hearsay, and speculation.

In the *disseminator* role, the manager passes some privileged information directly to subordinates, who would otherwise have no access to it. When subordinates lack easy contact with one another, the manager may pass information from one to another.

In the *spokesperson* role, the manager sends some information to people outside the unit—a president makes a speech to lobby for an organization cause, or a foreman suggests a product modification to a supplier. In addition, as a spokesperson, every manager must inform and satisfy the influential people who control the organizational unit. For the foreman, this may simply involve keeping the plant manager informed about the flow of work through the shop.

The president of a large corporation, however, may spend a great amount of time dealing with a host of

influences. Directors and shareholders must be advised
about finances; consumer groups must be assured that
the organization is fulfilling its social responsibilities;
and government officials must be satisfied that the organization is abiding by the law.

Decisional Roles

Information is not, of course, an end in itself; it is the
basic input to decision making. One thing is clear in the
study of managerial work: the manager plays the major
role in the unit's decision-making system. As its formal
authority, only the manager can commit the unit to
important new courses of action; and as its nerve center,
only the manager has full and current information to
make the set of decisions that determines the unit's
strategy. Four roles describe the manager as decision
maker.

As *entrepreneur*, the manager seeks to improve the
unit, to adapt it to changing conditions in the environment. In the monitor role, a president is constantly on
the lookout for new ideas. When a good one appears, he
initiates a development project that he may supervise
himself or delegate to an employee (perhaps with the
stipulation that he must approve the final proposal).

There are two interesting features about these development projects at the CEO level. First, these projects do
not involve single decisions or even unified clusters of
decisions. Rather, they emerge as a series of small decisions and actions sequenced over time. Apparently, chief
executives prolong each project both to fit it into a busy,
disjointed schedule, and so that they can comprehend
complex issues gradually.

Second, the chief executives I studied supervised as many as 50 of these projects at the same time. Some projects entailed new products or processes; others involved public relations campaigns, improvement of the cash position, reorganization of a weak department, resolution of a morale problem in a foreign division, integration of computer operations, various acquisitions at different stages of development, and so on.

Chief executives appear to maintain a kind of inventory of the development projects in various stages of development. Like jugglers, they keep a number of projects in the air; periodically, one comes down, is given a new burst of energy, and sent back into orbit. At various intervals, they put new projects on-stream and discard old ones.

While the entrepreneur role describes the manager as the voluntary initiator of change, the *disturbance handler* role depicts the manager involuntarily responding to pressures. Here change is beyond the manager's control. The pressures of a situation are too severe to be ignored—a strike looms, a major customer has gone bankrupt, or a supplier reneges on a contract—so the manager must act.

Leonard R. Sayles, who has carried out appropriate research on the manager's job, likens the manager to a symphony orchestra conductor who must "maintain a melodious performance,"[14] while handling musicians' problems and other external disturbances. Indeed, every manager must spend a considerable amount of time responding to high-pressure disturbances. No organization can be so well

The scarcest resource managers have to allocate is their own time.

run, so standardized, that it has considered every contingency in the uncertain environment in advance. Disturbances arise not only because poor managers ignore situations until they reach crisis proportions but also because good managers cannot possibly anticipate all the consequences of the actions they take.

The third decisional role is that of *resource allocator*. The manager is responsible for deciding who will get what. Perhaps the most important resource the manager allocates is his or her own time. Access to the manager constitutes exposure to the unit's nerve center and decision maker. The manager is also charged with designing the unit's structure, that pattern of formal relationships that determines how work is to be divided and coordinated.

Also, as resource allocator, the manager authorizes the important decisions of the unit before they are implemented. By retaining this power, the manager can ensure that decisions are interrelated. To fragment this power encourages discontinuous decision making and a disjointed strategy.

There are a number of interesting features about the manager's authorization of others' decisions. First, despite the widespread use of capital budgeting procedures—a means of authorizing various capital expenditures at one time—executives in my study made a great many authorization decisions on an ad hoc basis. Apparently, many projects cannot wait or simply do not have the quantifiable costs and benefits that capital budgeting requires.

Second, I found that the chief executives faced incredibly complex choices. They had to consider the impact of each decision on other decisions and on the organization's strategy. They had to ensure that the decision would be acceptable to those who influence the organization, as well as ensure that resources would not be overextended. They had to understand the various costs and benefits as well as the feasibility of the proposal. They also had to consider questions of timing. All this was necessary for the simple approval of someone else's proposal. At the same time, however, the delay could lose time, while quick approval could be ill-considered and quick rejection might discourage the subordinate who had spent months developing a pet project. One common solution to approving projects is to pick the person instead of the proposal. That is, the manager authorizes those projects presented by people whose judgment he or she trusts. But the manager cannot always use this simple dodge.

The final decisional role is that of *negotiator*. Managers spend considerable time in negotiations: the president of the football team works out a contract with the holdout superstar; the corporation president leads the company's contingent to negotiate a new strike issue; the foreman argues a grievance problem to its conclusion with the shop steward.

These negotiations are an integral part of the manager's job, for only he or she has the authority to commit organizational resources in "real time" and the nerve-center information that important negotiations require.

The Integrated Job

It should be clear by now that these ten roles are not easily separable. In the terminology of the psychologist, they form a gestalt, an integrated whole. No role can be pulled out of the framework and the job be left intact. For example, a manager without liaison contacts lacks external information. As a result, that manager can neither disseminate the information that employees need nor make decisions that adequately reflect external conditions. (This is a problem for the new person in a managerial position, since he or she has to build up a network of contacts before making effective decisions.)

Here lies a clue to the problems of team management.[15] Two or three people cannot share a single managerial position unless they can act as one entity. This means that they cannot divide up the ten roles unless they can very carefully reintegrate them. The real difficulty lies with the informational roles. Unless there can be full sharing of managerial information—and, as I pointed out earlier, it is primarily verbal—team management breaks down. A single managerial job cannot be arbitrarily split, for example, into internal and external roles, for information from both sources must be brought to bear on the same decisions.

To say that the ten roles form a gestalt is not to say that all managers give equal attention to each role. In fact, I found in my review of the various research studies that sales managers seem to spend relatively more of their time in the interpersonal roles, presumably a reflection of the extrovert nature of the marketing activity. Production managers, on the other hand, give relatively more attention to the decisional roles, presumably a reflection of their concern with efficient work flow. And staff managers spend the most time in the informational roles, since they are experts who manage departments that advise other parts of the organization. Nevertheless, in all cases, the interpersonal, informational, and decisional roles remain inseparable.

Toward More Effective Management

This description of managerial work should prove more important to managers than any prescription they might derive from it. That is to say, *the managers' effectiveness is significantly influenced by their insight into their own work.* Performance depends on how well a manager understands and responds to the pressures and dilemmas of the job. Thus managers who can be introspective about their work are likely to be effective at their jobs. The questions in "Self-Study Questions for Managers" on page 32 may sound rhetorical; none is meant to be. Even though the questions cannot be answered simply, the manager should address them.

Let us take a look at three specific areas of concern. For the most part, the managerial logjams—the dilemma of delegation, the database centralized in one brain, the problems of working with the management scientist—revolve around the verbal nature of the manager's information. There are great dangers in centralizing the organization's data bank in the minds of its managers. When they leave, they take their memory with them. And when subordinates are out of convenient verbal reach of the manager, they are at an informational disadvantage.

The manager is challenged to find systematic ways to share privileged information. A regular debriefing session with key subordinates, a weekly memory dump on the dictating machine, maintaining a diary for limited circulation, or other similar methods may ease the logjam of work considerably. The time spent disseminating this information will be more than regained when decisions must be made. Of course, some will undoubtedly raise the question of confidentiality. But managers would be well advised to weigh the risks of exposing privileged information against having subordinates who can make effective decisions.

If there is a single theme that runs through this article, it is that the pressures of the job drive the manager to take on too much work, encourage interruption, respond quickly to every stimulus, seek the tangible and avoid the abstract, make decisions in small increments, and do everything abruptly.

Here again, the manager is challenged to deal consciously with the pressures of superficiality by giving serious attention to the issues that require it, by stepping back in order to see a broad picture, and by making use of analytical inputs. Although effective managers have to be adept at responding quickly to numerous and varying problems, the danger in managerial work is that they will respond to every issue equally (and that means abruptly) and that they will never work the tangible bits and pieces of information into a comprehensive picture of their world.

To create this comprehensive picture, managers can supplement their own models with those of specialists. Economists describe the functioning of markets, operations researchers simulate financial flow processes, and behavioral scientists explain the needs and goals of people. The best of these models can be searched out and learned.

In dealing with complex issues, the senior manager has much to gain from a close relationship with the organization's own management scientists. They have something important that the manager lacks—time to probe complex issues. An effective working relationship hinges on the resolution of what a colleague and I have called "the planning dilemma."[16] Managers have the information and the authority; analysts have the time and the technology. A successful working relationship between the two will be effected when the manager learns to share information and the analyst learns to adapt to the manager's needs. For the analyst, adaptation means worrying less about the elegance of the method and more about its speed and flexibility.

Analysts can help the top manager schedule time, feed in analytical information, monitor projects, develop models to aid in making choices, design contingency plans for disturbances that can be anticipated, and conduct "quick and dirty" analyses for those that cannot. But there can be no cooperation if the analysts are out of the mainstream of the manager's information flow.

The manager is challenged to gain control of his or her own time by turning obligations into advantages and by turning those things he or she wishes to do into obligations. The chief executives of my study initiated only 32% of their own contacts (and another 5% by mutual agreement). And yet to a considerable extent they seemed to control their time. There were two key factors that enabled them to do so.

First, managers have to spend so much time discharging obligations that if they were to view them as just that, they would leave no mark on the organization. Unsuccessful managers blame failure on the obligations. Effective managers turn obligations to advantages. A speech is a chance to lobby for a cause; a meeting is a chance to reorganize a weak department; a visit to an important customer is a chance to extract trade information.

Second, the manager frees some time to do the things that he or she—perhaps no one else—thinks important by turning them into obligations. Free time is made, not found. Hoping to leave some time open for contemplation or general planning is tantamount to hoping that the pressures of the job will go away. Managers who want to innovate initiate projects and obligate others to report back to them. Managers who need certain environmental information establish channels that will automatically keep them informed. Managers who have to tour facilities commit themselves publicly.

The Educator's Job

Finally, a word about the training of managers. Our management schools have done an admirable job of training the organization's specialists—management scientists, marketing researchers, accountants, and organizational development specialists. But for the most part, they have not trained managers.[17]

Management schools will begin the serious training of managers when skill training takes a serious place next to cognitive learning. Cognitive learning is detached and informational, like reading a book or listening to a lecture. No doubt much important cognitive material must be assimilated by the manager-to-be. But cognitive learning no more makes a manager than it does a swimmer. The latter will drown the first time she jumps into the water if her coach never takes her out of the lecture hall, gets her wet, and gives her feedback on her performance.

In other words, we are taught a skill through practice plus feedback, whether in a real or a simulated situation. Our management schools need to identify the skills managers use, select students who show potential in these skills, put the students into situations where these skills can be practiced and developed, and then give them systematic feedback on their performance.

My description of managerial work suggests a number of important managerial skills—developing peer relationships, carrying out negotiations, motivating subordinates, resolving conflicts, establishing information networks and subsequently disseminating information, making decisions in conditions of extreme ambiguity, and allocating resources. Above all, the manager needs to be introspective in order to continue to learn on the job.

No job is more vital to our society than that of the manager. The manager determines whether our social institutions will serve us well or whether they will squander our talents and resources. It is time to strip away the folklore about managerial work and study it realistically so that we can begin the difficult task of making significant improvements in its performance.

Research on Managerial Work

IN SEEKING TO DESCRIBE MANAGERIAL WORK, I conducted my own research and scanned the literature to integrate the findings of studies from many diverse sources with my own. These studies focused on two different aspects of managerial work. Some were concerned with the characteristics of work—how long managers work, where, at what pace, with what interruptions, with whom they work, and through what media they communicate. Other studies were concerned with the content of work—what activities the managers actually carry out, and why. Thus, after a meeting, one researcher might note that the manager spent 45 minutes with three government officials in their Washington office, while another might record that the manager presented the company's stand on some proposed legislation in order to change a regulation.

A few of the studies of managerial work are widely known, but most have remained buried as single journal articles or isolated books. Among the more important ones I cite are:

- Sune Carlson developed the diary method to study the work characteristics of nine Swedish managing directors. Each kept a detailed log of his activities. Carlson's results are reported in his book *Executive Behaviour*. A number of British researchers, notably Rosemary Stewart, have subsequently used Carlson's method. In *Managers and Their Jobs*, she describes the study of 160 top and middle managers of British companies.

- Leonard Sayles's book *Managerial Behavior* is another important reference. Using a method he refers to as "anthropological," Sayles studied the work content of middle and lower level managers in a large U.S. corporation. Sayles moved freely in the company, collecting whatever information struck him as important.

- Perhaps the best-known source is *Presidential Power*, in which Richard Neustadt analyzes the power and managerial behavior of Presidents Roosevelt, Truman, and Eisenhower. Neustadt used secondary sources—documents and interviews with other parties.

- Robert H. Guest, in *Personnel,* reports on a study of the foreman's working day. Fifty-six U.S. foremen were observed and each of their activities recorded during one eight-hour shift.

- Richard C. Hodgson, Daniel J. Levinson, and Abraham Zaleznik studied a team of three top executives of a

U.S. hospital. From that study they wrote *The Executive Role Constellation*. They addressed the way in which work and socioemotional roles were divided among the three managers.

- William F. Whyte, from his study of a street gang during the Depression, wrote *Street Corner Society*. His findings about the gang's workings and leadership, which George C. Homans analyzed in *The Human Group*, suggest interesting similarities of job contents between street gang leaders and corporate managers.

My own study involved five American CEOs of middle- to large-sized organizations—a consulting firm, a technology company, a hospital, a consumer goods company, and a school system. Using a method called "structural observation," during one intensive week of observation for each executive, I recorded various aspects of every piece of mail and every verbal contact. In all, I analyzed 890 pieces of incoming and outgoing mail and 368 verbal contacts.

Retrospective Commentary

OVER THE YEARS, one reaction has dominated the comments I have received from managers who read "The Manager's Job: Folklore and Fact": "You make me feel so good. I thought all those other managers were planning, organizing, coordinating, and controlling, while I was busy being interrupted, jumping from one issue to another, and trying to keep the lid on the chaos." Yet everything in this article must have been patently obvious to these people. Why such a reaction to reading what they already knew?

Conversely, how to explain the very different reaction

of two media people who called to line up interviews after an article based on this one appeared in the *New York Times.* "Are we glad someone finally let managers have it," both said in passing, a comment that still takes me aback. True, they had read only the account in the *Times,* but that no more let managers have it than did this article. Why that reaction?

One explanation grows out of the way I now see this article—as proposing not so much another view of management as another face of it. I like to call it the insightful face, in contrast to the long-dominant professional or cerebral face. One stresses commitment, the other calculation; one sees the world with integrated perspective, the other figures it as the components of a portfolio. The cerebral face operates with the words and numbers of rationality; the insightful face is rooted in the images and feel of a manager's integrity.

Each of these faces implies a different kind of "knowing," and that, I believe, explains many managers' reaction to this article. Rationally, they "knew" what managers did—planned, organized, coordinated, and controlled. But deep down that did not feel quite right. The description in this article may have come closer to what they really "knew." As for those media people, they weren't railing against management as such but against the cerebral form of management, so pervasive, that they saw impersonalizing the world around them.

In practice, management has to be two-faced—there has to be a balance between the cerebral and the insightful. So, for example, I realized originally that managerial communication was largely oral and that the advent of the computer had not changed anything fundamental in the executive suite—a conclusion I continue to hold. (The greatest threat the personal computer poses is that managers will take it seriously and come to believe that they can manage by remaining in their offices and looking at displays of digital characters.) But I also thought that the dilemma of delegating could be dealt with by periodic debriefings—disseminating words. Now, however, I believe that managers need more ways to convey the images and impressions they carry inside of them. This explains the renewed interest in strategic vision, in culture, and in the roles of intuition and insight in management.

The ten roles I used to describe the manager's job also reflect management's cerebral face, in that they decompose the job more than capture the integration. Indeed, my effort to show a sequence among these roles now seems more consistent with the traditional face of management work than an insightful one. Might we not just as well say that people throughout the organization take actions that inform managers who, by making sense of those actions, develop images and visions that inspire people to subsequent efforts?

Perhaps my greatest disappointment about the research reported here is that it did not stimulate new efforts. In a world so concerned with management, much of the popular literature is superficial and the academic research pedestrian. Certainly, many studies have been carried out over the last 15 years, but the vast majority sought to replicate earlier research. In particular, we remain grossly ignorant about the fundamental content of the manager's job and have barely addressed the major issues and dilemmas in its practice.

But superficiality is not only a problem of the literature. It is also an occupational hazard of the manager's job. Originally, I believed this problem could be dealt with; now I see it as inherent in the job. This is because managing insightfully depends on the direct experience and personal knowledge that come from intimate contact. But in organizations grown larger and more diversified, that becomes difficult to achieve. And so managers turn increasingly to the cerebral face, and the delicate balance between the two faces is lost.

Certainly, some organizations manage to sustain their humanity despite their large size—as Tom Peters and Robert Waterman show in their book *In Search of Excellence*. But that book attained its outstanding success precisely because it is about the exceptions, about the organizations so many of us long to be a part of—not the organizations in which we actually work.

Fifteen years ago, I stated that "No job is more vital to our society than that of the manager. It is the manager who determines whether our social institutions serve us well or whether they squander our talents and resources." Now, more than ever, we must strip away the folklore of the manager's job and begin to face its difficult facts.

—Henry Mintzberg

Self-Study Questions for Managers

1. WHERE DO I GET MY INFORMATION, and how? Can I make greater use of my contacts? Can other people do some of my scanning? In what areas is my knowledge weakest, and how can I get others to provide me with the information I need? Do I have sufficiently powerful mental models of those things I must understand within the organization and in its environment?

2. What information do I disseminate? How important is that information to my subordinates? Do I keep too much information to myself because disseminating it is time consuming or inconvenient? How can I get more information to others so they can make better decisions?

3. Do I tend to act before information is in? Or do I wait so long for all the information that opportunities pass me by?

4. What pace of change am I asking my organization to tolerate? Is this change balanced so that our operations are neither excessively static nor overly disrupted? Have we sufficiently analyzed the impact of this change on the future of our organization?

5. Am I sufficiently well-informed to pass judgment on subordinate's proposals? Can I leave final authorization for more of the proposals with subordinates? Do we have problems of coordination because subordinates already make too many decisions independently?

6. What is my vision for this organization? Are these plans primarily in my own mind in loose form? Should I make them explicit to guide the decisions of others better? Or do I need flexibility to change them at will?

7. How do my subordinates react to my managerial style? Am I sufficiently sensitive to the powerful influence of my actions? Do I fully understand their reactions to my actions? Do I find an appropriate balance between encouragement and pressure? Do I stifle their initiative?

8. What kind of external relationships do I maintain, and how? Do I spend too much of my time maintaining them? Are there certain people whom I should get to know better?

9. Is there any system to my time scheduling, or am I just reacting to the pressures of the moment? Do I find the appropriate mix of activities or concentrate on one particular function or problem just because I find it interesting? Am I more efficient with particular kinds of work, at special times of the day or week? Does my schedule reflect this? Can someone else schedule my time (besides my secretary)?

10. Do I overwork? What effect does my work load have on my efficiency? Should I force myself to take breaks or to reduce the pace of my activity?

11. Am I too superficial in what I do? Can I really shift moods as quickly and frequently as my work requires? Should I decrease the amount of fragmentation and interruption in my work?

12. Do I spend too much time on current, tangible activities? Am I a slave to the action and excitement of my work, so that I am no longer able to concentrate on issues? Do key problems receive the attention they deserve? Should I spend more time reading and probing deeply into certain issues? Could I be more reflective? Should I be?

13. Do I use the different media appropriately? Do I know how to make the most of written communication? Do I rely excessively on face-to-face communication, thereby putting all but a few of my subordinates at an informational disadvantage? Do I schedule enough of my meetings on a regular basis? Do I spend enough time observing activities first-hand, or am I detached from the heart of my organization's activities?

14. How do I blend my personal rights and duties? Do my obligations consume all my time? How can I free myself from obligations to ensure that I am taking this organization where I want it to go? How can I turn my obligations to my advantage?

Notes

1. All the data from my study can be found in Henry Mintzberg, *The Nature of Managerial Work* (New York: Harper & Row, 1973).

2. Robert H. Guest, "Of Time and the Foreman," *Personnel*, May 1956, p. 478.

3. Rosemary Stewart, *Managers and Their Jobs* (London: Macmillan, 1967); see also Sune Carlson, *Executive Behavior* (Stockholm: Strombergs, 1951).

4. Francis J. Aguilar, *Scanning the Business Environment* (New York: Macmillan, 1967), p. 102.

5. Unpublished study by Irving Choran, reported in Mintzberg, *The Nature of Managerial Work*.

6. Robert T. Davis, *Performance and Development of Field Sales Managers* (Boston: Division of Research, Harvard Business School, 1957); George H. Copeman, *The Role of the Managing Director* (London: Business Publications, 1963

7. Stewart, *Managers and Their Jobs*; Tom Burns, "The Directions of Activity and Communication in a Departmental Executive Group," *Human Relations 7*, no. 1 (1954): 73.

8. H. Edward Wrapp, "Good Managers Don't Make Policy Decisions," HBR September–October 1967, p. 91. Wrapp refers to this as spotting opportunities and relationships in the stream of operating problems and decisions; in his article, Wrapp raises a number of excellent points related to this analysis.

9. Richard E. Neustadt, *Presidential Power* (New York: John Wiley, 1960), pp. 153-154; italics added.

10. For a more thorough, though rather different, discussion of this issue, see Kenneth R. Andrews, "Toward Professionalism in Business Management," HBR March–April 1969, p. 49.

11. C. Jackson Grayson, Jr., in "Management Science and Business Practice," HBR July–August 1973, p. 41, explains in similar terms why, as chairman of the Price Commis-

sion, he did not use those very techniques that he himself promoted in his earlier career as a management scientist.

12. George C. Homans, *The Human Group* (New York: Harcourt, Brace & World, 1950), based on the study by William F. Whyte entitled *Street Corner Society*, rev. ed. (Chicago: University of Chicago Press, 1955).

13. Neustadt, *Presidential Power*, p. 157.

14. Leonard R. Sayles, *Managerial Behavior* (New York: McGraw-Hill, 1964), p. 162.

15. See Richard C. Hodgson, Daniel J. Levinson, and Abraham Zaleznik, *The Executive Role Constellation* (Boston: Division of Research, Harvard Business School, 1965), for a discussion of the sharing of roles.

16. James S. Hekimian and Henry Mintzberg, "The Planning Dilemma," *The Management Review*, May 1968, p. 4.

17. See J. Sterling Livingston, "Myth of the Well-Educated Manager," HBR January–February 1971, p.79.

Originally published in July–August 1975
Reprint 90210

This article won the McKinsey Award for excellence and was reprinted in HBR in March–April 1990.

What Leaders Really Do

JOHN P. KOTTER

Executive Summary

LEADERSHIP IS DIFFERENT FROM MANAGEMENT, but not for the reasons most people think. Leadership isn't mystical and mysterious. It has nothing to do with having "charisma" or other exotic personality traits. It is not the province of a chosen few. Nor is leadership necessarily better than management or a replacement for it.

Rather, leadership and management are two distinctive and complementary systems of action. Each has its own function and characteristic activities. Both are necessary for success in today's business environment.

Management is about coping with complexity. Its practices and procedures are largely a response to the emergence or large, complex organizations in the twentieth century. Leadership, by contrast, is about coping with change. Part of the reason it has become so important in recent years is that the business world has become more competitive and more volatile. More change always demands more leadership.

Most U.S. corporations today are overmanaged and underled. They need to develop their capacity to exercise leadership. Successful corporations don't wait for leaders to come along. They actively seek out people with leadership potential and expose them to career experiences designed to develop that potential. Indeed, with careful selection, nurturing, and encouragement, dozens of people can play important leadership roles in a business organization.

But while improving their ability to lead, companies should remember that strong leadership with weak management is no better, and is sometimes actually worse, than the reverse. The real challenge is to combine strong leadership and strong management and use each to balance the other.

LEADERSHIP IS DIFFERENT FROM MANAGEMENT, but not for the reasons most people think. Leadership isn't mystical and mysterious. It has nothing to do with having "charisma" or other exotic personality traits. It is not the province of a chosen few. Nor is leadership necessarily better than management or a replacement for it.

Rather, leadership and management are two distinctive and complementary systems of action. Each has its own function and characteristic activities. Both are necessary for success in an increasingly complex and volatile business environment.

Most U.S. corporations today are overmanaged and underled. They need to develop their capacity to exercise leadership. Successful corporations don't wait for leaders to come along. They actively seek out people with leader-

Leadership complements management; it doesn't replace it.

ship potential and expose them to career experiences designed to develop that potential. Indeed, with careful selection, nurturing, and encouragement, dozens of people can play important leadership roles in a business organization.

But while improving their ability to lead, companies should remember that strong leadership with weak management is no better, and is sometimes actually worse, than the reverse. The real challenge is to combine strong leadership and strong management and use each to balance the other.

Of course, not everyone can be good at both leading and managing. Some people have the capacity to become excellent managers but not strong leaders. Others have great leadership potential but, for a variety of reasons, have great difficulty becoming strong managers. Smart companies value both kinds of people and work hard to make them a part of the team.

But when it comes to preparing people for executive jobs, such companies rightly ignore the recent literature that says people cannot manage *and* lead. They try to develop leader-managers. Once companies understand the fundamental difference between leadership and management, they can begin to groom their top people to provide both.

The Difference Between Management and Leadership

Management is about coping with complexity. Its practices and procedures are largely a response to one of the most significant developments of the twentieth century: the emergence of large organizations. Without good management, complex enterprises tend to become chaotic in ways that threaten their very existence. Good management brings a degree of order and consistency to key dimensions like the quality and profitability of products.

Leadership, by contrast, is about coping with change. Part of the reason it has become so important in recent years is that the business world has become more competitive and more volatile. Faster technological change, greater international competition, the deregulation of markets, overcapacity in capital-intensive industries, an unstable oil cartel, raiders with junk bonds, and the changing demographics of the work force are among the many factors that have contributed to this shift. The net result is that doing what was done yesterday, or doing it 5% better, is no longer a formula for success. Major changes are more and more necessary to survive and compete effectively in this new environment. More change always demands more leadership.

Consider a simple military analogy: a peacetime army can usually survive with good administration and management up and down the hierarchy, coupled with good leadership concentrated at the very top. A wartime army, however, needs competent leadership at all levels. No one yet has figured out how to manage people effectively into battle; they must be led.

These different functions—coping with complexity and coping with change—shape the characteristic activities of management and leadership. Each system of action involves deciding what needs to be done, creating networks of people and relationships that can accomplish an agenda, and then trying to ensure that those people actually do the job. But each accomplishes these three tasks in different ways.

Companies manage complexity first by *planning and budgeting*—setting targets or goals for the future (typically for the next month or year), establishing detailed steps for achieving those targets, and then allocating resources to accomplish those plans. By contrast, leading an organization to constructive change begins by *setting a direction*—developing a vision of the future (often the distant future) along with strategies for producing the changes needed to achieve that vision.

Management develops the capacity to achieve its plan by *organizing and staffing*—creating an organizational structure and set of jobs for accomplishing plan requirements, staffing the jobs with qualified individuals, communicating the plan to those people, delegating responsibility for carrying out the plan, and devising systems to monitor implementation. The equivalent leadership activity, however, is *aligning people*. This means communicating the new direction to those who can create coalitions that understand the vision and are committed to its achievement.

Finally, management ensures plan accomplishment by *controlling and problem solving*—monitoring results versus the plan in some detail, both formally and informally, by means of reports, meetings, and other tools; identifying deviations; and then planning and organizing to solve the problems. But for leadership, achieving a vision requires *motivating and inspiring*—keeping people moving in the right direction, despite major obstacles to change, by appealing to basic but often untapped human needs, values, and emotions.

A closer examination of each of these activities will help clarify the skills leaders need.

Setting a Direction vs. Planning and Budgeting

Since the function of leadership is to produce change, setting the direction of that change is fundamental to leadership.

Setting direction is never the same as planning or even long-term planning, although people often confuse the two. Planning is a management process, deductive in nature and designed to produce orderly results, not change. Setting a direction is more inductive. Leaders gather a broad range of data and look for patterns, relationships, and linkages that help explain things. What's more, the direction-setting aspect of leadership does not produce plans; it creates vision and strategies. These describe a business, technology, or corporate culture in terms of what it should become over the long term and articulate a feasible way of achieving this goal.

Most discussions of vision have a tendency to degenerate into the mystical. The implication is that a vision is something mysterious that mere mortals, even talented ones, could never hope to have. But developing good business direction isn't magic. It is a tough, sometimes exhausting process of gathering and analyzing information. People who articulate such visions aren't magicians but broadbased strategic thinkers who are willing to take risks.

Nor do visions and strategies have to be brilliantly innovative; in fact, some of the best are not. Effective business visions regularly have an almost mundane quality, usually consisting of ideas that are already well known. The particular combination or patterning of the ideas may be new, but sometimes even that is not the case.

For example, when CEO Jan Carlzon articulated his vision to make Scandinavian Airline Systems (SAS) the best airline in the world for the frequent business traveler, he was not saying anything that everyone in the airline industry didn't already know. Business travelers fly more consistently than other market segments and are generally willing to pay higher fares. Thus focusing on business customers offers an airline the possibility of high margins, steady business, and considerable growth. But in an industry known more for bureaucracy than vision, no company had ever put these simple ideas together and dedicated itself to implementing them. SAS did, and it worked.

What's crucial about a vision is not its originality but how well it serves the interests of important constituencies—customers, stockholders, employees—and how easily it can be translated into a realistic competitive strategy. Bad visions tend to ignore the legitimate needs and rights of important constituencies—favoring, say, employees over customers or stockholders. Or they are strategically unsound. When a company that has never been better than a weak competitor in an industry suddenly starts talking about becoming number one, that is a pipe dream, not a vision.

One of the most frequent mistakes that overmanaged and underled corporations make is to embrace "long-term planning" as a panacea for their lack of direction and inability to adapt to an increasingly competitive and dynamic business environment. But such an approach misinterprets the nature of direction setting and can never work.

Long-term planning is always time consuming. Whenever something unexpected happens, plans have to be redone. In a dynamic business environment, the unexpected often becomes the norm, and long-term planning can become an extraordinarily burdensome activity. This is why most successful corporations limit the time frame of their planning activities. Indeed, some even consider "long-term planning" a contradiction in terms.

In a company without direction, even short-term planning can become a black hole capable of absorbing an infinite amount of time and energy. With no vision and strategy to provide constraints around the planning process or to guide it, every eventuality deserves a plan. Under these circumstances, contingency planning can go on forever, draining time and attention from far more essential activities, yet without ever providing the clear sense of direction that a company desperately needs. After awhile, managers inevitably become cynical about all this, and the planning process can degenerate into a highly politicized game.

Planning works best not as a substitute for direction setting but as a complement to it. A competent planning process serves as a useful reality check on direction-setting activities. Likewise, a competent direction-setting process provides a focus in which planning can then be realistically carried out. It helps clarify what kind of planning is essential and what kind is irrelevant. (See "Setting Direction: Lou Gerstner at American Express" on page 53.)

Aligning People vs. Organizing and Staffing

A central feature of modern organizations is interdependence, where no one has complete autonomy, where most employees are tied to many others by their work, technology, management systems, and hierarchy. These linkages present a special challenge when organizations attempt to change. Unless many individuals line up and move together in the same direction, people will tend to fall all over one another. To executives who are overeducated in management and undereducated in leadership, the idea of getting people moving in the same direction appears to be an organizational problem. What executives need to do, however, is not organize people but align them.

Managers "organize" to create human systems that can implement plans as precisely and efficiently as possible. Typically, this requires a number of potentially complex decisions. A company must choose a structure of jobs and reporting relationships, staff it with individuals suited to the jobs, provide training for those who need it, communicate plans to the work force, and decide how much authority to delegate and to whom. Economic incentives also need to be constructed to accomplish the plan, as well as systems to monitor its implementation. These organizational judgments are much like architectural decisions. It's a question of fit within a particular context.

Aligning is different. It is more of a communications challenge than a design problem. First, aligning invariably involves talking to many more individuals than organizing does. The target population can involve not only a manager's subordinates but also bosses, peers, staff in other parts of the organization, as well as suppliers, governmental officials, or even customers. Anyone who can help implement the vision and strategies or who can block implementation is relevant.

Trying to get people to comprehend a vision of an alternative future is also a communications challenge of a completely different magnitude from organizing them to fulfill a short-term plan. It's much like the difference between a football quarterback attempting to describe to his team the next two or three plays versus his trying to explain to them a totally new approach to the game to be used in the second half of the season.

Whether delivered with many words or a few carefully chosen symbols, such messages are not necessarily accepted just because they are understood. Another big challenge in leadership efforts is credibility—getting people to believe the message. Many things contribute to credibility: the track record of the person delivering the message, the content of the message itself, the communicator's reputation for integrity and trustworthiness, and the consistency between words and deeds.

Finally, aligning leads to empowerment in a way that organizing rarely does. One of the reasons some organizations have difficulty adjusting to rapid changes in markets or technology is that so many people in those companies feel relatively powerless. They have learned from experience that even if they correctly perceive important external changes and then initiate appropriate actions, they are vulnerable to someone higher up who does not like what they have done. Reprimands can take many different forms: "That's against policy" or "We can't afford it" or "Shut up and do as you're told."

Alignment helps overcome this problem by empowering people in at least two ways. First, when a clear sense of direction has been communicated throughout an organization, lower level employees can initiate actions without the same degree of vulnerability. As long as their behavior is consistent with the vision, superiors will have more difficulty reprimanding them. Second, because everyone is aiming at the same target, the probability is less that one person's initiative will be stalled when it comes into conflict with someone else's. (See "Aligning People: Chuck Trowbridge and Bob Crandall at Eastman Kodak" on page 56.)

Motivating People vs. Controlling and Problem Solving

Since change is the function of leadership, being able to generate highly energized behavior is important for coping with the inevitable barriers to change. Just as direction setting identifies an appropriate path for movement and just as effective alignment gets people moving down that path, successful motivation ensures that they will have the energy to overcome obstacles.

According to the logic of management, control mechanisms compare system behavior with the plan and take action when a deviation is detected. In a well-managed factory, for example, this means the planning process establishes sensible quality targets, the organizing process builds an organization that can achieve those targets, and a control process makes sure that quality lapses are spotted immediately, not in 30 or 60 days, and corrected.

Management controls people by pushing them in the right direction; leadership motivates them by satisfying basic human needs.

For some of the same reasons that control is so central to management, highly motivated or inspired behavior is almost irrelevant. Managerial processes must be as close as possible to fail-safe and risk-free. That means they cannot be dependent on the unusual or hard to obtain. The whole purpose of systems and structures is to help normal people who behave in normal ways to complete routine jobs successfully, day after day. It's not exciting or glamorous. But that's management.

Leadership is different. Achieving grand visions always requires an occasional burst of energy. Motivation and inspiration energize people, not by pushing them in the right direction as control mechanisms do but by satisfying basic human needs for achievement, a sense of belonging, recognition, self-esteem, a feeling of control over one's life, and the ability to live up to one's ideals. Such feelings touch us deeply and elicit a powerful response.

Good leaders motivate people in a variety of ways. First, they always articulate the organization's vision in a manner that stresses the values of the audience they are addressing. This makes the work important to those individuals. Leaders also regularly involve people in deciding how to achieve the organization's vision (or the part most relevant to a particular individual). This gives people a sense of control. Another important motivational technique is to support employee efforts to realize the vision by providing coaching, feedback, and role modeling, thereby helping people grow professionally and enhancing their self-esteem. Finally, good leaders recognize and reward success, which not only gives people a sense of accomplishment but also makes them feel like they belong to an organization that cares about them. When all this is done, the work itself becomes intrinsically motivating.

The more that change characterizes the business environment, the more that leaders must motivate people to provide leadership as well. When this works, it tends to reproduce leadership across the entire organization, with people occupying multiple leadership roles throughout the hierarchy. This is highly valuable, because coping with change in any complex business demands initiatives from a multitude of people. Nothing less will work.

Of course, leadership from many sources does not necessarily converge. To the contrary, it can easily conflict. For multiple leadership roles to work together, people's actions must be carefully coordinated by mechanisms that differ from those coordinating traditional management roles.

Strong networks of informal relationships—the kind found in companies with healthy cultures—help coordinate leadership activities in much the same way that formal structure coordinates managerial activities. The key difference is that informal networks can deal with the greater demands for coordination associated with nonroutine activities and change. The multitude of communication channels and the trust among the individuals connected by those channels allow for an ongoing process of accommodation and adaptation. When conflicts arise among roles, those same relationships help resolve the conflicts. Perhaps most important, this process of dialogue and accommodation can produce visions that are linked and compatible instead of remote and competitive. All this requires a great deal more communication than is needed to coordinate managerial roles, but unlike formal structure, strong informal networks can handle it.

Of course, informal relations of some sort exist in all corporations. But too often these networks are either very weak—some people are well connected but most are not—or they are highly fragmented—a strong network exists inside the marketing group and inside R&D but not across the two departments. Such networks do not support multiple leadership initiatives well. In fact, extensive informal networks are so important that if they do not exist, creating them has to be the focus of activity early in a major leadership initiative. (See "Motivating People: Richard Nicolosi at Procter & Gamble" on page 58.)

Creating a Culture of Leadership

Despite the increasing importance of leadership to business success, the on-the-job experiences of most people actually seem to undermine the development of attributes needed for leadership. Nevertheless, some companies have consistently demonstrated an ability to develop people into outstanding leader-managers. Recruiting people with leadership potential is only the first step. Equally important is managing their career patterns. Individuals who are effective in large leadership roles often share a number of career experiences.

Perhaps the most typical and most important is significant challenge early in a career. Leaders almost always have had opportunities during their twenties and thirties to actually try to lead, to take a risk, and to learn from both triumphs and failures. Such learning seems essential in developing a wide range of leadership skills and perspectives.

Despite leadership's growing importance, the on-the-job experiences of most people undermine their ability to lead.

It also teaches people something about both the difficulty of leadership and its potential for producing change.

Later in their careers, something equally important happens that has to do with broadening. People who provide effective leadership in important jobs always have a chance, before they get into those jobs, to grow beyond the narrow base that characterizes most managerial careers. This is usually the result of lateral career moves or of early promotions to unusually broad job assignments. Sometimes other vehicles help, like special task-force assignments or a lengthy general management course. Whatever the case, the breadth of knowledge developed in this way seems to be helpful in all aspects of leadership. So does the network of relationships that is often acquired both inside and outside the company. When enough people get opportunities like this, the relationships that are built also help create the strong informal networks needed to support multiple leadership initiatives.

One way to develop leadership is to create challenging opportunities for young employees.

Corporations that do a better-than-average job of developing leaders put an emphasis on creating challenging opportunities for relatively young employees. In many businesses, decentralization is the key. By definition, it pushes responsibility lower in an organization and in the process creates more challenging jobs at lower levels. Johnson & Johnson, 3M, Hewlett-Packard, General Electric, and many other well-known companies have used that approach quite successfully. Some of those same companies also create as many small units as possible so there are a lot of challenging lower level general management jobs available.

Sometimes these businesses develop additional challenging opportunities by stressing growth through new products or services. Over the years, 3M has had a policy that at least 25% of its revenue should come from products introduced within the last five years. That encourages small new ventures, which in turn offer hundreds of opportunities to test and stretch young people with leadership potential.

Such practices can, almost by themselves, prepare people for small- and medium-sized leadership jobs. But developing people for important leadership positions requires more work on the part of senior executives, often over a long period of time. That work begins with efforts to spot people with great leadership potential early in their careers and to identify what will be needed to stretch and develop them.

Again, there is nothing magic about this process. The methods successful companies use are surprisingly straightforward. They go out of their way to make young employees and people at lower levels in their organizations visible to senior management. Senior managers then judge for themselves who has potential and what the development needs of those people are. Executives also discuss their tentative conclusions among themselves to draw more accurate judgments.

Armed with a clear sense of who has considerable leadership potential and what skills they need to develop, executives in these companies then spend time planning for that development. Sometimes that is done as part of a formal succession planning or high-potential development process; often it is more informal. In either case, the key ingredient appears to be an intelligent assessment of what feasible development opportunities fit each candidate's needs.

To encourage managers to participate in these activities, well-led businesses tend to recognize and reward people who successfully develop leaders. This is rarely done as part of a formal compensation or bonus formula, simply because it is so difficult to measure such achievements with precision. But it does become a fac-

Institutionalizing a leadership-centered culture is the ultimate act of leadership.

tor in decisions about promotion, especially to the most senior levels, and that seems to make a big difference. When told that future promotions will depend to some degree on their ability to nurture leaders, even people who say that leadership cannot be developed somehow find ways to do it.

Such strategies help create a corporate culture where people value strong leadership and strive to create it. Just as we need more people to provide leadership in the complex organizations that dominate our world today, we also need more people to develop the cultures that will create that leadership. Institutionalizing a leadership-entered culture is the ultimate act of leadership.

Setting Direction: Lou Gerstner at American Express

WHEN LOU GERSTNER BECAME PRESIDENT of the Travel Related Services (TRS) arm at American Express in 1979, the unit was facing one of its biggest challenges in AmEx's 130-year history. Hundreds of banks were offering or planning to introduce credit cards through Visa and MasterCard that would compete with the American Express card. And more than two dozen financial service firms were coming into the traveler's checks business. In a mature marketplace, this increase in competition usually reduces margins and prohibits growth.

But that was not how Gerstner saw the business. Before joining American Express, he had spent five years as a consultant to TRS, analyzing the money-losing travel division and the increasingly competitive card operation. Gerstner and his team asked fundamental questions about the economics, market, and competition and developed a deep understanding of the business. In the process, he began to craft a vision of TRS that looked nothing like a 130-year-old company in a mature industry.

Gerstner thought TRS had the potential to become a dynamic and growing enterprise, despite the onslaught of Visa and MasterCard competition from thousands of banks. The key was to focus on the global marketplace and, specifically, on the relatively affluent customer American Express had been traditionally serving with top-of-the-line products. By further segmenting this market, aggressively developing a broad range of new products and services, and investing to increase productivity and to lower costs, TRS could provide the best service possible to customers who had enough discretionary income to buy many more services from TRS than they had in the past.

Within a week of his appointment, Gerstner brought together the people running the card organization and questioned all the principles by which they conducted their business. In particular, he challenged two widely shared beliefs—that the division should have only one product, the green card, and that this product was limited in potential for growth and innovation.

Gerstner also moved quickly to develop a more entrepreneurial culture, to hire and train people who would thrive in it, and to clearly communicate to them the overall direction. He and other top managers rewarded intelligent risk taking. To make entrepreneurship easier, they discouraged unnecessary bureaucracy. They also upgraded hiring standards and created the TRS Graduate Management Program, which offered high-potential young people special training, an enriched set of experiences, and an unusual degree of exposure to people in top management. To encourage risk taking among all TRS employees, Gerstner also established something called the Great Performers program to recognize and reward truly exceptional customer service, a central tenet in the organization's vision.

These incentives led quickly to new markets, products, and services. TRS expanded its overseas presence dramatically. By 1988, AmEx cards were issued in 29 currencies (as opposed to only 11 a decade earlier). The unit also focused aggressively on two market segments that had historically received little attention: college students and women. In 1981, TRS combined its card and travel-service capabilities to offer corporate clients a unified system to monitor and control travel expenses. And by 1988, AmEx had grown to become the fifth largest direct-mail merchant in the United States.

Other new products and services included 90-day insurance on all purchases made with the AmEx card, a Platinum American Express card, and a revolving credit card known as Optima. In 1988, the company also switched to image-processing technology for billing, producing a more convenient monthly statement for customers and reducing billing costs by 25%.

As a result of these innovations, TRS's net income increased a phenomenal 500% between 1978 and 1987—a compounded annual rate of about 18%. The business outperformed many so-called high-tech/high-growth companies. With a 1988 return on equity of 28%, it also outperformed most low-growth but high-profit businesses.

Aligning People: Chuck Trowbridge and Bob Crandall at Eastman Kodak

EASTMAN KODAK ENTERED THE COPY BUSINESS IN THE EARLY 1970s, concentrating on technically sophisticated machines that sold, on average, for about $60,000 each. Over the next decade, this business grew to nearly $1 billion in revenues. But costs were high, profits were hard to find, and problems were nearly everywhere. In 1984, Kodak had to write off $40 million in inventory.

Most people at the company knew there were problems, but they couldn't agree on how to solve them. So, in his first two months as general manager of the new copy products group, established in 1984, Chuck Trowbridge met with nearly every key person inside his group, as well as with people elsewhere at Kodak who could be important to the copier business. An especially crucial area was the engineering and manufacturing organization, headed by Bob Crandall.

Trowbridge and Crandall's vision for engineering and manufacturing was simple: to become a world-class manufacturing operation and to create a less bureaucratic and more decentralized organization. Still, this message was difficult to convey because it was such a radical departure from previous communications, not only in the copy products group but throughout most of Kodak. So Crandall set up dozens of vehicles to emphasize the new direction and align people to it: weekly meetings with his own 12 direct reports; monthly "copy product forums" in which a different employee from each of his departments would meet with him as a group; discuss recent improvements and new projects to achieve still better results; and quarterly "State of the Department" meetings, where his managers met with everybody in their own departments.

Once a month, Crandall and all those who reported to him would also meet with 80 to 100 people from some area of his organization to discuss anything they wanted. To align his biggest supplier—the Kodak Apparatus Division, which supplied one-third of the parts used in design and manufacturing—he and his managers met with the top management of that group over lunch every Thursday. More recently, he has created a format called "business meetings," where his managers meet with 12 to 20 people on a specific topic, such as inventory or master scheduling. The goal is to get all of his 1,500 employees in at least one of these focused business meetings each year.

Trowbridge and Crandall also enlisted written communication in their cause. A four-to eight-page "Copy Products Journal" was sent to employees once a month. A program called "Dialog Letters" gave employees the opportunity to anonymously ask questions of Crandall and his top managers and be guaranteed a reply. But the most visible, and powerful, form of written communication were the charts. In a main hallway near the cafeteria, these huge charts vividly reported the quality, cost, and delivery results for each product, measured against difficult targets. A hundred smaller versions of these charts were scattered throughout the manufacturing area, reporting quality levels and costs for specific work groups.

Results of this intensive alignment process began to appear within six months and still more after a year. These successes made the message more credible and helped get more people on board. Between 1984 and 1988, quality on one of the main product lines increased nearly one-hundredfold. Defects per unit went from 30 to 0.3.

Over a three-year period, costs on another product line went down nearly 24%. Deliveries on schedule increased from 82% in 1985 to 95% in 1987. Inventory levels dropped by over 50% between 1984 and 1988, even though the volume of products was increasing. And productivity, measured in units per manufacturing employee, more than doubled between 1985 and 1988.

Motivating People: Richard Nicolosi at Procter & Gamble

FOR ABOUT 20 YEARS SINCE ITS FOUNDING IN 1956, Procter & Gamble's paper products division had experienced little competition for its high-quality, reasonably priced, and well-marketed consumer goods. By the late 1970s, however, the market position of the division had changed. New competitive thrusts hurt P&G badly. For example, industry analysts estimate that the company's market share for disposable diapers fell from 75% in the mid-1970s to 52% in 1984.

That year, Richard Nicolosi came to paper products as the associate general manager, after three years in P&G's smaller and faster moving soft-drink business. He found a heavily bureaucratic and centralized organization that was overly preoccupied with internal functional goals and projects. Almost all information about customers came through highly quantitative market research. The technical people were rewarded for cost savings, the commercial people focused on volume and share, and the two groups were nearly at war with each other.

During the late summer of 1984, top management announced that Nicolosi would become the head of paper products in October, and by August he was unofficially running the division. Immediately he began to stress the need for the division to become more creative and market driven, instead of just trying to be a low-cost producer. "I had to make it very clear," Nicolosi later reported, "that the rules of the game had changed."

The new direction included a much greater stress on teamwork and multiple leadership roles. Nicolosi pushed a strategy of using groups to manage the division and its specific products. In October, he and his team designated themselves as the paper division "board" and began meeting first monthly and then weekly. In November, they established "category teams" to manage their major brand groups (like diapers, tissues, towels) and started pushing responsibility down to these teams. "Shun the incremental," Nicolosi stressed, "and go for the leap."

In December, Nicolosi selectively involved himself in more detail in certain activities. He met with the advertising agency and got to know key creative people. He asked the marketing manager of diapers to report directly to him, eliminating a layer in the hierarchy. He talked more to the people who were working on new product-development projects.

In January 1985, the board announced a new organizational structure that included not only category teams but also new-brand business teams. By the spring, the board was ready to plan an important motivational event to communicate the new paper products vision to as many people as possible. On June 4, 1985, all the Cincinnati-based personnel in paper plus sales district managers and paper plant managers—several thousand people in all—met in the local Masonic Temple. Nicolosi and other board members described their vision of an organization where "each of us is a leader." The event was videotaped, and an edited version was sent to all sales offices and plants for everyone to see.

All these activities helped create an entrepreneurial environment where large numbers of people were motivated to realize the new vision. Most innovations came from people dealing with new products. Ultra Pampers, first introduced in February 1985, took the market share of the entire Pampers product line from 40% to 58% and profitability from break-even to positive. And within only a few months of the introduction of Luvs Delux in May 1987, market share for the overall brand grew by 150%.

Other employee initiatives were oriented more toward a functional area, and some came from the bottom of the hierarchy. In the spring of 1986, a few of the division's secretaries, feeling empowered by the new culture, developed a Secretaries network. This association established subcommittees on training, on rewards and recognition, and on the "secretary of the future." Echoing the sentiments of many of her peers, one paper products secretary said: "I don't see why we too can't contribute to the division's new direction."

By the end of 1988, revenues at the paper products division were up 40% over a four-year period. Profits were up 68%. And this happened despite the fact that the competition continued to get tougher.

Originally published in May–June 1990
Reprint 90309

Managers and Leaders

Are They Different?

ABRAHAM ZALEZNIK

Executive Summary

MANAGERS AND LEADERS are two very different types of people. Managers' goals arise out of necessities rather than desires; they excel at diffusing conflicts between individuals or departments, placating all sides while ensuring that an organization's day to day business gets done. Leaders, on the other hand, adopt personal, active attitudes towards goals. They look for the potential opportunities and rewards that lie around the corner, inspiring subordinates and firing up the creative process with their own energy. Their relationships with employees and coworkers are intense, and their working environment is often, consequently chaotic.

Businesses need both managers and leaders to survive and succeed. But in larger U.S. organizations, a "managerial mystique" seems to have taken hold that perpetuates the development of managerial personalities—

people who rely on, and strive to maintain, orderly, stable, work patterns. The managerial power ethic favors collective leadership and seeks to avoid risk.

That same "managerial mystique" stifles the development of leaders—how can an entrepreneurial spirit develop when it is submerged in a conservative environment and denied personal attention? Mentor relationships are crucial to the development of leadership personalities, but in large, bureaucratic organizations, such relationships are not encouraged.

Businesses must find ways to train good managers and develop leaders at the same time. Without a solid organizational framework, even leaders with the most brilliant of ideas may spin their wheels, frustrating coworkers and accomplishing little. But without the entrepreneurial culture that develops when a leader is at the helm of an organization, a business will stagnate, and rapidly lose competitive power.

WHAT IS THE IDEAL WAY TO DEVELOP LEADERSHIP? Every society provides its own answer to this question, and each, in groping for answers, defines its deepest concerns about the purposes, distributions, and uses of power. Business has contributed its answer to the leadership question by evolving a new breed called the manager. Simultaneously, business has established a new power ethic that favors collective over individual leadership, the cult of the group over that of personality. While ensuring the competence, control, and the balance of power among groups with the potential for rivalry, managerial leadership unfortunately does not necessarily ensure imagination, creativity, or ethical behavior in guiding the destinies of corporate enterprises.

Leadership inevitably requires using power to influence the thoughts and actions of other people. Power in the hands of an individual entails human risks: first, the risk of equating power with the ability to get immediate results; second, the risk of ignoring the many different ways people can legitimately accumulate power; and third, the risk of losing self-control in the desire for power. The need to hedge these risks accounts in part for the development of collective leadership and the managerial ethic. Consequently, an inherent conservatism dominates the culture of large organizations. In *The Second American Revolution,* John D. Rockefeller III describes the conservatism of organizations: "An organization is a system, with a logic of its own, and all the weight of tradition and inertia. The deck is stacked in favor of the tried and proven way of doing things and against the taking of risks and striking out in new directions."[1]

Out of this conservatism and inertia, organizations provide succession to power through the development of managers rather than individual leaders. Ironically, this ethic fosters a bureaucratic culture in business, supposedly the last bastion protecting us from the encroachments and controls of bureaucracy in government and education.

Manager vs. Leader Personality

A managerial culture emphasizes rationality and control. Whether his or her energies are directed toward goals, resources, organization structures, or people, a manager is a problem solver. The manager asks: "What problems have to be solved, and what are the best ways to achieve results so that people will continue to contribute to this organization?" From this perspective, leadership is simply a practical effort to direct affairs; and to fulfill his or her task, a manager requires that many people operate efficiently at different levels of status and responsibility. It takes neither genius nor heroism to be a manager, but rather persistence, tough-mindedness, hard work, intelligence, analytical ability, and perhaps most important, tolerance and goodwill.

Another conception of leadership, however, attaches almost mystical beliefs to what a leader is and assumes that only great people are worthy of the drama of power and politics. Here leadership is a psychodrama in which a brilliant, lonely person must gain control of himself or herself as a precondition for controlling others. Such an expectation of leadership contrasts sharply with the mundane, practical, and yet important conception that leadership is really managing work that other people do.

Two questions come to mind. Is this leadership mystique merely a holdover from our childhood—from a sense of dependency and a longing for good and heroic parents? Or is it true that no matter how competent managers are, their leadership stagnates because of their limitations in visualizing purposes and generating value in work? Driven by narrow purposes, without an imaginative capacity and the ability to communicate, do managers then perpetuate group conflicts instead of reforming them into broader desires and goals?

What it takes to develop managers may inhibit developing leaders.

If indeed problems demand greatness, then judging by past performance, the selection and development of leaders leave a great deal to chance. There are no known ways to train "great" leaders. Further, beyond what we leave to chance, there is a deeper issue in the relationship between the need for competent managers and the longing for great leaders.

What it takes to ensure a supply of people who will assume practical responsibility may inhibit the development of great leaders. On the other hand, the presence of great leaders may undermine the development of managers who typically become very anxious in the relative disorder that leaders seem to generate.

It is easy enough to dismiss the dilemma of training managers, though we may need new leaders or leaders at the expense of managers, by saying that the need is for people who can be both. But just as a managerial culture differs from the entrepreneurial culture that develops when leaders appear in organizations, managers and leaders are very different kinds of people. They differ in motivation, personal history, and in how they think and act. (See "Retrospective Commentary" on page 83.)

Attitudes Toward Goals

Managers tend to adopt impersonal, if not passive, attitudes toward goals. Managerial goals arise out of necessities rather than desires and, therefore, are deeply embedded in their organization's history and culture.

Frederic G. Donner, chairman and chief executive officer of General Motors from 1958 to 1967, expressed this kind of attitude toward goals in defining GM's position on product development:

"To meet the challenge of the marketplace, we must recognize changes in customer needs and desires far enough ahead to have the right products in the right places at the right time and in the right quantity.

"We must balance trends in preference against the many compromises that are necessary to make a final product that is both reliable and good looking, that performs well and that sells at a competitive price in the necessary volume. We must design not just the cars we would like to build but, more important, the cars that our customers want to buy."[2]

Nowhere in this statement is there a notion that consumer tastes and preferences arise in part as a result of what manufacturers do. In reality, through product design, advertising, and promotion, consumers learn to like what they then say they need. Few would argue that people who enjoy taking snapshots need a camera that also develops pictures. But in response to a need for novelty, convenience, and a shorter interval between acting (snapping the picture) and gaining pleasure (seeing the shot), the Polaroid camera succeeded in the marketplace. It is inconceivable that Edwin Land responded to impressions of consumer need. Instead, he translated a technology (polarization of light) into a product, which proliferated and stimulated consumers' desires.

Edwin Land didn't just respond to consumer needs. He stimulated consumer desires.

The example of Polaroid and Land suggests how leaders think about goals. They are active instead of reactive, shaping ideas instead of responding to them. Leaders adopt a personal and active attitude toward goals. The influence a leader exerts in altering moods, evoking images and expectations, and in establishing specific desires and objectives determines the direction a business takes. The net result of this influence changes the way people think about what is desirable, possible, and necessary.

Conceptions of Work

Managers tend to view work as an enabling process involving some combination of people and ideas interacting to establish strategies and make decisions. They help the process along by calculating the interests in opposition, planning when controversial issues should surface, and reducing tensions. In this enabling process, managers' tactics appear flexible: on one hand, they negotiate and bargain; on the other, they use rewards, punishments, and other forms of coercion.

Alfred P. Sloan's actions at General Motors illustrate how this process works in situations of conflict. The time was the early 1920s when Ford Motor Company still dominated the automobile industry using, as did General Motors, the conventional water-cooled engine. With the full backing of Pierre du Pont, Charles Kettering dedicated himself to the design of an air-cooled copper engine, which, if successful, would be a great technical and marketing coup for GM. Kettering believed in his product, but the manufacturing division heads opposed the new design on two grounds: first, it was technically unreliable, and second, the corporation was putting all its eggs in one basket by investing in a new product instead of attending to the current marketing situation.

In the summer of 1923, after a series of false starts and after its decision to recall the copper engine Chevrolets from dealers and customers, GM management scrapped the project. When it dawned on Kettering that the company had rejected the engine, he was deeply discouraged and wrote to Sloan that, without the "organized resistance" against the project, it would have succeeded and that, unless the project were saved, he would leave the company.

Alfred Sloan was all too aware that Kettering was unhappy and indeed intended to leave General Motors. Sloan was also aware that, while the manufacturing divisions strongly opposed the new engine, Pierre du Pont supported Kettering. Further, Sloan had himself gone on record in a letter to Kettering less than two years earlier expressing full confidence in him. The problem Sloan had was how to make his decision stick, keep Kettering in the organization (he was much too valuable to lose), avoid alienating du Pont, and encourage the division heads to continue developing product lines using conventional water-cooled engines.

Sloan's actions in the face of this conflict reveal much about how managers work. First, he tried to reassure Kettering by presenting the problem in a very ambiguous fashion, suggesting that he and the executive committee sided with Kettering, but that it would not be practical to force the divisions to do what they were opposed to. He presented the problem as being a question of the people, not the product. Second, he proposed to reorganize around the problem by consolidating all functions in a new division that would be responsible for the design, production, and marketing of the new engine. This solution appeared as ambiguous as his efforts to placate Kettering. Sloan wrote: "My plan was to create an independent pilot operation under the sole jurisdiction of Mr. Kettering, a kind of copper-cooled car division. Mr. Kettering would designate his own chief engineer and his production staff to solve the technical problems of manufacture."[3]

Sloan did not discuss the practical value of this solution, which included saddling an inventor with management responsibility, but in effect, he used this plan to limit his conflict with Pierre du Pont.

Essentially, the managerial solution that Sloan arranged limited the options available to others. The structural solution narrowed choices, even limiting emotional reactions to the point where the key people could do nothing but go along. It allowed Sloan to say in his memorandum to du Pont, "We have discussed the matter with Mr. Kettering at some length this morning, and he agrees with us absolutely on every point we made. He appears to receive the suggestion enthusiastically and has every confidence that it can be put across along these lines."[4]

Sloan placated people who opposed his views by developing a structural solution that appeared to give something but in reality only limited options. He could then authorize the car division's general manager, with whom he basically agreed, to move quickly in designing water-cooled cars for the immediate market demand.

Years later, Sloan wrote, evidently with tongue in cheek, "The copper-cooled car never came up again in a big way. It just died out; I don't know why."[5]

To get people to accept solutions to problems, managers continually need to coordinate and balance opposing views. Interestingly enough, this type of work has much in common with what diplomats and mediators do, with Henry Kissinger apparently an outstanding practitioner. Managers aim to shift balances of power toward solutions acceptable as compromises among conflicting values.

Leaders work in the opposite direction. Where managers act to limit choices, leaders develop fresh approaches to long-standing problems and open issues to new options. To be effective, leaders must project their ideas onto images that excite people and only then develop choices that give those images substance.

John F. Kennedy's brief presidency shows both the strengths and weaknesses connected with the excitement leaders generate in their work. In his inaugural address he said, "Let every nation know, whether it wishes us well or ill, that we shall pay any price, bear any burden, meet any hardship, support any friend, oppose any foe, in order to assure the survival and the success of liberty."

This much-quoted statement forced people to react beyond immediate concerns and to identify with Kennedy and with important shared ideals. On closer scrutiny, however, the statement is absurd because it promises a position, which, if adopted, as in the Vietnam War, could produce disastrous results. Yet unless expectations are aroused and mobilized, with all the dangers of frustration inherent in heightened desire, new thinking and new choice can never come to light.

Leaders work from high-risk positions; indeed, they are often temperamentally disposed to seek out risk and danger, especially where the chance of opportunity and reward appears promising. From my observations, the reason one individual seeks risks while another approaches problems conservatively depends more on his or her personality and less on conscious choice. For those who become managers, a survival instinct dominates the need for risk, and with that instinct comes an ability to tolerate mundane, practical work. Leaders sometimes react to mundane work as to an affliction.

Relations with Others

Managers prefer to work with people; they avoid solitary activity because it makes them anxious. Several years ago, I directed studies on the psychological aspects of careers. The need to seek out others with whom to work and collaborate seemed to stand out as an important characteristic of managers. When asked, for example, to write imaginative stories in response to a picture showing a single figure (a boy contemplating a violin or a man silhouetted in a state of reflection), managers populated their stories with people. The following is an example of a manager's imaginative story about the young boy contemplating a violin:

"Mom and Dad insisted that their son take music lessons so that someday he can become a concert musician. His instrument was ordered and had just arrived. The boy is weighing the alternatives of playing football with the other kids or playing with the squeak box. He can't understand how his parents could think a violin is better than a touchdown.

"After four months of practicing the violin, the boy has had more than enough, Dad is going out of his mind, and Mom is willing to give in reluctantly to their wishes. Football season is now over, but a good third baseman will take the field next spring."

This story illustrates two themes that clarify managerial attitudes toward human relations. The first, as I have suggested, is to seek out activity with other people (that is, the football team), and the second is to maintain a low level of emotional involvement in those relationships. Low emotional involvement appears in the writer's use of conventional metaphors, even clichés, and in the depiction of the ready transformation of potential conflict into harmonious decisions. In this case, the boy, Mom, and Dad agree to give up the violin for sports.

These two themes may seem paradoxical, but their coexistence supports what a manager does, including reconciling differences, seeking compromises, and establishing a balance of power. The story further demonstrates that managers may lack empathy, or the capacity to sense intuitively the thoughts and feelings of others. Consider another story written to the same stimulus picture by someone thought of as a leader by his peers:

"This little boy has the appearance of being a sincere artist, one who is deeply affected by the violin, and has an intense desire to master the instrument.

"He seems to have just completed his normal practice session and appears to be somewhat crestfallen at his inability to produce the sounds that he is sure lie within the violin.

"He appears to be in the process of making a vow to himself to expend the necessary time and effort to play this instrument until he satisfies himself that he is able to bring forth the qualities of music that he feels within himself.

"With this type of determination and carry-through, this boy became one of the great violinists of his day."

Empathy is not simply a matter of paying attention to other people. It is also the capacity to take in emotional signals and make them meaningful in a relationship. People who describe another person as "deeply affected," with "intense desire," "crestfallen," and as one who can "vow to himself" would seem to have an inner perceptiveness that they can use in their relationships with others.

Managers relate to people according to the role they play in a sequence of events or in a decision-making process, while leaders, who are concerned with ideas, relate in more intuitive and empathetic ways. The distinction is simply between a manager's attention to *how* things get done and a leader's to *what* the events and decisions mean to participants.

In recent years, managers have adopted from game theory the notion that decision-making events can be one of two types: the win-lose situation (or zero-sum game) or the win-win situation in which everybody in the action comes out ahead. Managers strive to convert win-lose into win-win situations as part of the process of reconciling differences among people and maintaining balances of power.

As an illustration, take the decision of how to allocate capital resources among operating divisions in a large, decentralized organization. On the surface, the dollars available for distribution are limited at any given time. Presumably, therefore, the more one division gets, the less is available for other divisions.

Managers tend to view this situation (as it affects human relations) as a conversion issue: how to make what seems like a win-lose problem into a win-win problem. From that perspective, several solutions come to mind. First, the manager focuses others' attention on procedure and not on substance. Here the players become engrossed in the bigger problem of *how* to make decisions, not *what* decisions to make. Once committed to the bigger problem, these people have to support the outcome since they were involved in formulating the decision-making rules. Because they believe in the rules they formulated, they will accept present losses, believing that next time they will win.

Second, the manager communicates to subordinates indirectly, using "signals" instead of "messages." A signal holds a number of implicit positions, while a message clearly states a position. Signals are inconclusive and subject to reinterpretation should people become upset and angry; messages involve the direct consequence that some people will indeed not like what they hear. The nature of messages heightens emotional response and makes managers anxious. With signals, the question of who wins and who loses often becomes obscured.

Third, the manager plays for time. Managers seem to recognize that with the passage of time and the delay of major decisions, compromises emerge that take the sting out of win-lose situations, and the original "game" will be superseded by additional situations. Compromises mean that one may win and lose simultaneously, depending on which of the games one evaluates.

There are undoubtedly many other tactical moves managers use to change human situations from win-lose to win-win. But the point is that such tactics focus on the decision-making process itself, and that process interests managers rather than leaders. Tactical interests involve costs as well as benefits; they make organizations fatter in bureaucratic and political intrigue and leaner in direct, hard activity and warm human relationships.

Leader's lives are marked by a continual struggle to attain some sense of order.

Consequently, one often hears subordinates characterize managers as inscrutable, detached, and manipulative. These adjectives arise from the subordinates' perception that they are linked together in a process whose purpose is to maintain a controlled as well as rational and equitable structure.

In contrast, one often hears leaders referred to with adjectives rich in emotional content. Leaders attract strong feelings of identity and difference or of love and hate. Human relations in leader-dominated structures often appear turbulent, intense, and at times even disorganized. Such an atmosphere intensifies individual motivation and often produces unanticipated outcomes.

Senses of Self

In *The Varieties of Religious Experience*, William James describes two basic personality types, "once-born" and "twice-born." People of the former personality type are those for whom adjustments to life have been straightforward and whose lives have been more or less a peaceful flow since birth. Twice-borns, on the other hand, have not had an easy time of it. Their lives are marked by a continual struggle to attain some sense of order. Unlike once-borns, they cannot take things for granted. According to James, these personalities have equally different worldviews. For a once-born personality, the sense of self as a guide to conduct and attitude derives from a feeling of being at home and in harmony with one's environment. For a twice-born, the sense of self derives from a feeling of profound separateness.

A sense of belonging or of being separate has a practical significance for the kinds of investments managers and leaders make in their careers. Managers see themselves as conservators and regulators of an existing order of affairs with which they personally identify and from which they gain rewards. A manager's sense of self-worth is enhanced by perpetuating and strengthening existing institutions: he or she is performing in a role that harmonizes with ideals of duty and responsibility.

William James had this harmony in mind—this sense of self as flowing easily to and from the outer world—in defining a once-born personality.

Leaders tend to be twice-born personalities, people who feel separate from their environment. They may work in organizations, but they never belong to them. Their sense of who they are does not depend on memberships, work roles, or other social indicators of identity. And that perception of identity may form the theoretical basis for explaining why certain individuals seek opportunities for change. The methods to bring about change may be technological, political, or ideological, but the object is the same: to profoundly alter human, economic, and political relationships.

In considering the development of leadership, we have to examine two different courses of life history: (1) development through socialization, which prepares the individual to guide institutions and to maintain the existing balance of social relations; and (2) development through personal mastery, which impels an individual to struggle for psychological and social change. Society produces its managerial talent through the first line of development; leaders emerge through the second.

Development of Leadership

Every person's development begins with family. Each person experiences the traumas associated with separating from his or her parents, as well as the pain that follows such a wrench. In the same vein, all individuals face the difficulties of achieving self-regulation and self-control. But for some, perhaps a majority, the fortunes of childhood provide adequate gratifications and sufficient opportunities to find substitutes for rewards no longer available. Such individuals, the "once-borns," make moderate identifications with parents and find a harmony between what they expect and what they are able to realize from life.

But suppose the pains of separation are amplified by a combination of parental demands and individual needs to the degree that a sense of isolation, of being special, or of wariness disrupts the bonds that attach children to parents and other authority figures? Given a special aptitude under such conditions, the person becomes deeply involved in his or her inner world at the expense of interest in the outer world. For such a person, self-esteem no longer depends solely on positive attachments and real rewards. A form of self-reliance takes hold along with expectations of performance and achievement, and perhaps even the desire to do great works.

Such self-perceptions can come to nothing if the individual's talents are negligible. Even with strong talents, there are no guarantees that achievement will follow, let alone that the end result will be for good rather than evil. Other factors enter into development as well. For one, leaders are like artists and other gifted people who often struggle with neuroses; their ability to function varies considerably even over the short run, and some potential leaders lose the struggle altogether. Also, beyond early childhood, the development patterns that affect managers and leaders involve the selective influence of particular people. Managerial personalities form moderate and widely distributed attachments. Leaders, on the other hand, establish, and also break off, intensive one-to-one relationships.

It is a common observation that people with great talents are often indifferent students. No one, for example, could have predicted Einstein's great achievements on the basis of his mediocre record in school. The reason for mediocrity is obviously not the absence of ability. It may result, instead, from self-absorption and the inability to pay attention to the ordinary tasks at hand. The only sure way an individual can interrupt reverie-like preoccupation and self-absorption is to form a deep attachment to a great teacher or other person who understands and has the ability to communicate with the gifted individual.

Gifted people need one-to-one relationships. Eisenhower had General Connor, Carnegie had Thomas Scott.

Whether gifted individuals find what they need in one-to-one relationships depends on the availability of teachers, possibly parental surrogates, whose strengths lie in cultivating talent. Fortunately, when generations meet and the self-selections occur, we learn more about how to develop leaders and how talented people of different generations influence each other.

While apparently destined for mediocre careers, people who form important one-to-one apprenticeship relationships often are able to accelerate and intensify their development. The psychological readiness of an individual to benefit from such a relationship depends on some experience in life that forces that person to turn inward.

Consider Dwight Eisenhower, whose early career in the army foreshadowed very little about his future development. During World War I, while some of his West Point classmates were already experiencing the war firsthand in France, Eisenhower felt "embedded in the monotony and unsought safety of the Zone of the Interior . . . that was intolerable punishment."[1]

Shortly after World War I, Eisenhower, then a young officer somewhat pessimistic about his career chances, asked for a transfer to Panama to work under General Fox Connor, a senior officer whom he admired. The army turned down his request. This setback was very much on Eisenhower's mind when Ikey, his first born son, succumbed to influenza. Through some sense of responsibility for its own, the army then transferred Eisenhower to Panama, where he took up his duties under General Connor with the shadow of his lost son very much upon him.

In a relationship with the kind of father he would have wanted to be, Eisenhower reverted to being the son he had lost. And in this highly charged situation, he began to learn from his teacher. General Connor offered, and Eisenhower gladly took, a magnificent tutorial on the military. The effects of this relationship on Eisenhower cannot be measured quantitatively, but in examining his career path from that point, one cannot overestimate its significance.

As Eisenhower wrote later about Connor, "Life with General Connor was a sort of graduate school in military affairs and the humanities, leavened by a man who was experienced in his knowledge of men and their conduct. I can never adequately express my gratitude to this one gentleman. . . . In a lifetime of association with great and good men, he is the one more or less invisible figure to whom I owe an incalculable debt."[7]

Some time after his tour of duty with General Connor, Eisenhower's breakthrough occurred. He received orders to attend the Command and General Staff School at Fort Leavenworth, one of the most competitive schools in the army. It was a coveted appointment, and Eisenhower took advantage of the opportunity. Unlike his performance in high school and West Point, his work at the Command School was excellent; he was graduated first in his class.

Psychological biographies of gifted people repeatedly demonstrate the important part a teacher plays in developing an individual. Andrew Carnegie owed much to his senior, Thomas A. Scott. As head of the Western Division of the Pennsylvania Railroad, Scott recognized talent and the desire to learn in the young telegrapher assigned to him. By giving Carnegie increasing responsibility and by providing him with the opportunity to learn through close personal observation, Scott added to Carnegie's self-confidence and sense of achievement. Because of his own personal strength and achievement, Scott did not fear Carnegie's aggressiveness. Rather, he gave it full play in encouraging Carnegie's initiative.

Great teachers take risks. They bet initially on talent they perceive in younger people. And they risk emotional involvement in working closely with their juniors. The risks do not always pay off, but the willingness to take them appears to be crucial in developing leaders.

Can Organizations Develop Leaders?

A myth about how people learn and develop that seems to have taken hold in American culture also dominates thinking in business. The myth is that people learn best from their peers. Supposedly, the threat of evaluation and even humiliation recedes in peer relations because of the tendency for mutual identification and the social restraints on authoritarian behavior among equals. Peer training in organizations occurs in various forms. The use, for example, of task forces made up of peers from several interested occupational groups (sales, production, research, and finance) supposedly removes the restraints of authority on the individual's willingness to assert and exchange ideas. As a result, so the theory goes, people interact more freely, listen more objectively to criticism and other points of view, and, finally, learn from this healthy interchange.

Another application of peer training exists in some large corporations, such as Philips N.V. in Holland, where organizational structure is built on the principle of joint responsibility of two peers, one representing the commercial end of the business and the other the technical. Formally, both hold equal responsibility for geographic operations or product groups, as the case may be. As a practical matter, it may turn out that one or the other of the peers dominates the management. Nevertheless, the main interaction is between two or more equals.

The principal question I raise about such arrangements is whether they perpetuate the managerial orientation and preclude the formation of one-to-one relationships between senior people and potential leaders.

Aware of the possible stifling effects of peer relationships on aggressiveness and individual initiative, another company, much smaller than Philips, utilizes joint responsibility of peers for operating units, with one important difference. The chief executive of this company encourages competition and rivalry among peers, ultimately rewarding the one who comes out on top with increased responsibility. These hybrid arrangements produce some unintended consequences that can be disastrous. There is no easy way to limit rivalry. Instead, it permeates all levels of the operation and opens the way for the formation of cliques in an atmosphere of intrigue.

One large, integrated oil company has accepted the importance of developing leaders through the direct influence of senior on junior executives. The chairman and chief executive officer regularly selects one talented university graduate whom he appoints his special assistant, and with whom he will work closely for a year. At the end of the year, the junior executive becomes available for assignment to one of the operating divisions, where he or she will be assigned to a responsible post rather than a training position. This apprenticeship acquaints the junior executive firsthand with the use of power and with the important antidotes to the power disease called *hubris*—performance and integrity.

Working in one-to-one relationships, where there is a formal and recognized difference in the power of the players, takes a great deal of tolerance for emotional interchange. This interchange, inevitable in close working arrangements, probably accounts for the reluctance of many executives to become involved in such relationships. *Fortune* carried an interesting story on the departure of a key executive, John W. Hanley, from the top management of Procter & Gamble to the chief executive officer position at Monsanto.[8] According to this account, the chief executive and chairman of P & G passed over Hanley for appointment to the presidency, instead naming another executive vice president to this post.

The chairman evidently felt he could not work well with Hanley who, by his own acknowledgment, was aggressive, eager to experiment and change practices, and constantly challenged his superior. A chief executive officer naturally has the right to select people with whom he feels congenial. But I wonder whether a greater capacity on the part of senior officers to tolerate the competitive impulses and behavior of their subordinates might not be healthy for corporations. At least a greater tolerance for interchange would not favor the managerial team player at the expense of the individual who might become a leader.

I am constantly surprised at the frequency with which chief executives feel threatened by open challenges to their ideas, as though the source of their authority, rather than their specific ideas, was at issue. In one case, a chief executive officer, who was troubled by the aggressiveness and sometimes outright rudeness of one of his talented vice presidents, used various indirect methods such as group meetings and hints from outside directors to avoid dealing with his subordinate. I advised the executive to deal head-on with what irritated him. I suggested that by direct, face-to-face confrontation, both he and his subordinate would learn to validate the distinction between the authority to be preserved and the issues to be debated.

The ability to confront is also the ability to tolerate aggressive interchange. And that skill not only has the net effect of stripping away the veils of ambiguity and signaling so characteristic of managerial cultures, but also it encourages the emotional relationships leaders need if they are to survive.

Retrospective Commentary

IT WAS NOT SO LONG AGO that Bert Lance, President Jimmy Carter's budget director and confidant, declared, "If it ain't broke, don't fix it." This piece of advice fits with how managers think. Leaders understand a different truth: "When it ain't broke may be the only time you can fix it."

In the splendid discipline of the marketplace, past formulas for success today contain the seeds of decay. The U.S. automobile industry has been cited so often as the prime example of the suicidal effect of continuing to do what one has been doing in the wake of success that its story borders on the banal. But it's true. Top executives in the automobile industry, along with managers in many other industries in the United States, have failed to understand the misleading lessons of success, revealing the chronic fault of the managerial mystique.

As a consequence of placing such reliance on the practical measure of continuing to do today and tomorrow what had proved successful yesterday, we face the chilling fact that the United States's largest export during the last decade or more has been jobs. We live with the grim reality that the storehouse of expertise called know-how has diminished. Perhaps most dismal of all, our children and our children's children may not be able to enjoy the same standard of living we worked so hard to achieve, let alone enjoy a higher standard of living as a legacy of the generations.

When "Managers and Leaders: Are They Different?" first appeared in HBR, practicing managers and academics, including many of my colleagues at the Harvard Business School, thought I had taken leave of my senses. Don't ordinary people in an organization with superior structure and process outperform superior people operating in an ordinary organization? To those indoctrinated in the "managerial mystique," talent is ephemeral while organization structure and process are real. The possibility that it takes talent to make a company hum counts for less than acting on those variables managers feel they understand and can control.

Talent is critical to continued success in the marketplace. Yet most organizations today persist in perpetuating the development of managers over leaders. Fortunately, however, there may be an awakening. The chairman of IBM, John Akers, startled the business community with his announcement that IBM intended to abandon its long-held course of running its business as one large corporation. Akers intends to break IBM up into a number of corporations. And while "Big Blue" will continue to be big by most standards, the businesses will run under a leadership and not a managerial mentality. The corporation will no longer rest on the false comforts of economy of scale. Nor will executives be preoccupied with coordination and control, with decentralized operations and centralized financial controls. Process will take a backseat to substance, and the power will flow to executives who are creative and, above all, aggressive.

If other large companies follow this lead, corporate America may recharge, and its ability to compete may rebound. But if left to professional management, U.S. corporations will continue to stagnate.

Since "Managers and Leaders: Are They Different?" was first published, strategy has catapulted itself into the number one position on the managerial hit parade. No aspect of corporate life is indifferent to strategy. Every problem leads to strategic solutions, ranging from how to position products to how to compensate executives. We have a plethora of marketing strategies, employee benefit strategies, and executive development strategies. Strategy, it seems, has replaced business policy as the conceptual handle for establishing a corporation's directives.

In relying on strategy, organizations have largely overlooked results. Strategy is an offspring of the branch of economics called industrial organization; it builds models of competition and attempts to position products in competitive markets through analytic techniques. The aggregation of these product positions establishes mission statements and direction for businesses. With the ascendancy of industrial organization in the 1980s, management consultants prospered and faith in the managerial mystique was strengthened, despite the poor performance in the U.S. economy.

To me, the most influential development in management in the last 10 or 15 years has been Lotus 1-2-3. This popular software program makes it possible to create spreadsheets rapidly and repetitively, and that has given form and language to strategic planning. With this methodology, technicians can play with the question, "What if?" Best of all, everyone with access to a computer and the appropriate software can join in the "what if" game.

Alas, while everyone can become a strategist, few can become, and sustain, the position of creator. Vision, the hallmark of leadership, is less a derivative of spreadsheets and more a product of the mind called imagination.

And vision is needed at least as much as strategy to succeed. Business leaders bring to bear a variety of imaginations on the growth of corporations. These imaginations—the marketing imagination, the manufacturing imagination, and others—originate in perceptual capacities we recognize as talent. Talented leaders grasp the significance of anomalies, such as unfulfilled customer needs, manufacturing operations that can be improved significantly, and the potential of technological applications in product development.

Business imaginations are substantive. A leader's imagination impels others to act in ways that are truly, to use James MacGregor Burns's felicitous term, "transformational." But leaders often experience their talent as restlessness, as a desire to upset other people's applecarts, an impelling need to "do things better." As a consequence, a leader may not create a stable working environment; rather, he or she may create a chaotic workplace, with highly charged emotional peaks and valleys.

In "Managers and Leaders: Are They Different?", I argued that a crucial difference between managers and leaders lies in the conceptions they hold, deep in their psyches, of chaos and order. Leaders tolerate chaos and lack of structure and are thus prepared to keep answers in suspense, avoiding premature closure on important issues. Managers seek order and control and are almost compulsively addicted to disposing of problems even before they understand their potential significance. In my experience, seldom do the uncertainties of potential chaos cause problems. Instead, it is the instinctive move to impose order on potential chaos that makes trouble for organizations.

It seems to me that business leaders have much more in common with artists, scientists, and other creative thinkers than they do with managers. For business schools to exploit this commonality of dispositions and interests, the curriculum should worry less about the logics of strategy and imposing the constraints of computer exercises and more about thought experiments in the play of creativity and imagination. If they are successful, they would then do a better job of preparing exceptional men and women for positions of leadership.

—Abraham Zaleznik

Notes

1. New York: Harper & Row, 1973, p. 72.

2. Alfred P. Sloan, Jr., *My Years with General Motors* (New York: Doubleday, 1964), p. 440.

3. Ibid., p. 91.

4. Ibid.

5. Ibid., p. 93.

6. Dwight D. Eisenhower, *At Ease: Stories I Tell To Friends* (New York: Doubleday, 1967), p. 136.

7. Ibid., p. 187.

8. "Jack Hanley Got There by Selling Harder," *Fortune*, November 1976.

Originally published in May–June 1977
Reprint 92211

This article was reprinted in HBR *in March–April 1992.*

The Discipline of Building Character

JOSEPH L. BADARACCO, JR.

Executive Summary

WHAT IS THE DIFFERENCE BETWEEN an ethical decision and what the author calls a *defining moment*? An ethical decision typically involves choosing between two options: one we know to be right and another we know to be wrong. A defining moment challenges us in a deeper way by asking us to choose between two or more ideals in which we deeply believe. Such decisions rarely have one "correct" response. Taken cumulatively over many years, they form the basis of an individual's character.

Defining moments ask executives to dig below the busy surface of their lives and refocus on their core values and principles. Once uncovered, those values and principles renew their sense of purpose at the workplace and act as a springboard for shrewd, pragmatic, politically astute action. Three types of defining moments

89

are particularly common in today's workplace. The first type is largely an issue of personal identity. It raises the question, Who am I? The second type concerns groups as well as individuals. It raises the question, Who are we? The third kind involves defining a company's role within society. It raises the question, Who is the company?

By learning to identify each of those three situations, managers can learn to navigate right-versus-right decisions successfully. The author asks a series of practical questions that will help managers take time out to examine their values and then transform their beliefs into action. By engaging in this process of self-inquiry, managers will be gaining the tools to tackle their most elusive, challenging, and essential business dilemmas.

W E HAVE ALL EXPERIENCED, at one time or another, situations in which our professional responsibilities unexpectedly come into conflict with our deepest values. A budget crisis forces us to dismiss a loyal, hardworking employee. Our daughter has a piano recital on the same afternoon that our biggest client is scheduled to visit our office. At these times, we are caught in a conflict between right and right. And no matter which option we choose, we feel like we've come up short.

Managers respond to these situations in a variety of ways: some impulsively "go with their gut"; others talk it over with their friends, colleagues, or families; still others think back to what a mentor would do in similar circumstances. In every case, regardless of what path is chosen, these decisions taken cumulatively over many years form the very basis of an individual's character. For that reason, I call them *defining moments.*

What is the difference between a tough ethical decision and a defining moment? An ethical decision typically involves choosing between two options: one we know to be right and another we know to be wrong. A defining moment, however, challenges us in a deeper way by asking us to choose between two or more ideals in which we deeply believe. Such challenges rarely have a "correct" response. Rather, they are situations created by circumstance that ask us to step forward and, in the words of the American philosopher John Dewey, "form, reveal, and test" ourselves. We form our character in defining moments because we commit to irreversible courses of action that shape our personal and professional identities. We reveal something new about us to ourselves and others because defining moments uncover something that had been hidden or crystallize something that had been only partially known. And we test ourselves because we discover whether we will live up to our personal ideals or only pay them lip service.

As I have interviewed and studied business leaders, I have found that the ones who are most satisfied with the way they resolve their defining moments possess skills that are left off most job descriptions. Specifically, they are able to take time out from the chain of managerial tasks that consumes their time and undertake a process of probing self-inquiry—a process that is more often carried out on the run rather than in quiet seclusion. They are able to dig below the busy surface of their daily lives and refocus on their core

To become leaders, managers need to translate their personal values into calculated action.

values and principles. Once uncovered, those values and principles renew their sense of purpose at work and act as a springboard for shrewd, pragmatic, politically astute action. By repeating this process again and again throughout their work lives, these executives are able to craft an authentic and strong identity based on their own, rather than on someone else's, understanding of what is right. And in this way, they begin to make the transition from being a manager to becoming a leader.

But how can an executive trained in the practical, extroverted art of management learn to engage in such an intuitive, personal process of introspection? In this article, I will describe a series of down-to-earth questions that will help managers take time out from the hustle and bustle of the workplace. These practical, thought-provoking questions are designed to transform values and beliefs into calculated action. They have been drawn from well-known classic and contemporary philosophers but remain profound and flexible enough to embrace a wide range of contemporary right-versus-right decisions. By taking time out to engage in this process of self-inquiry, managers will by no means be conducting a fruitless exercise in escapism; rather, they will be getting a better handle on their most elusive, challenging, and essential business problems.

In today's workplace, three kinds of defining moments are particularly common. The first type is largely an issue of personal identity. It raises the question, Who am I? The second type is organizational as well as personal: both the character of groups within an organization and the character of an individual manager are at stake. It raises the question, Who are we? The third type of defining moment is the most complex and involves defining a company's role in society. It raises

the question, Who is the company? By learning to identify each of these three defining moments, managers will
learn to navigate right-versus-right decisions with grace
and strength. (See "A Guide to Defining Moments" on
page 112.)

Who am I? Defining Moments for Individuals

The most basic type of defining moment demands that
managers resolve an urgent issue of personal identity
that has serious implications for their careers. Two
"rights" present themselves, each one representing a
plausible and usually attractive life choice. And therein
lies the problem: there is no one right answer; right is set
against right.

CONFLICTING FEELINGS

When caught in this bind, managers can begin by taking
a step back and looking at the conflict not as a problem
but as a natural tension between two valid perspectives.
To flesh out this tension, we can ask, *What feelings and
intuitions are coming into conflict in this situation?* As
Aristotle discussed in his classic work *Ethics*, people's
feelings can actually help them make sense of an issue,
understand its basic dimensions, and indicate what the
stakes really are. In other words, our feelings and intuitions are both a form of intelligence and a source of
insight.

Consider, for example, the case of a young analyst—
we will call him Steve Lewis—who worked for a well-
known investment bank in Manhattan.[1] Early one morning, Lewis, an African-American, found a message on his

desk asking if he could fly to St. Louis in two days to help with a presentation to an important prospective client. The message came as a surprise to him. Lewis's company had a clear policy against including analysts in presentations or client meetings. Lewis, in fact, knew little about the subject of the St. Louis meeting, which concerned a specialized area of municipal finance. He was especially surprised to learn that he had been selected over more senior people in the public finance group.

Lewis immediately walked down the hall into the office of his friend and mentor, also an African-American, and asked him if he knew about the situation. His friend, a partner at the company, replied, "Let me tell you what's happening, Steve. Look at you and me. What do we have in common? Did you know that the new state treasurer of Missouri is also black? I hate for you to be introduced to this side of the business so soon, but the state treasurer wants to see at least one black professional at the meeting or else the company has no chance of being named a manager for this deal."

What if at this point Lewis were to step back and reframe the situation in terms of his feelings and intuitions? On the one hand, Lewis believed firmly that in order to maintain his self-respect, he had to earn his advancement at the company—and elsewhere in life. He was not satisfied to move up the ladder of success based on affirmative action programs or being a "token" member of the company. For that reason, he had always wanted to demonstrate through his work that he deserved his position. On the other hand, as a former athlete, Lewis had always prided himself on being a team player and did not believe in letting his teammates down. By examining his feelings and intuitions about the situation, Lewis learned that the issue at hand was more complex than whether or not to go to the presentation. It involved a conflict between two of his most deeply held beliefs.

DEEPLY ROOTED VALUES

By framing defining moments in terms of our feelings and intuitions, we can remove the conflict from its business context and bring it to a more personal, and manageable, level. Then we can consider a second question to help resolve the conflict: *Which of the responsibilities and values that are in conflict are most deeply rooted in my life and in the communities I care about?* Tracing the roots of our values means understanding their origins and evolution over time. It involves an effort to understand which values and commitments really mean the most to us.

Let's apply that approach to the case of Steve Lewis. On the one hand, he had no doubt that he wanted to become a partner at a major investment bank and that he wanted to earn that position based on merit. Since his sophomore year of college, Lewis had been drawn to the idea of a career on Wall Street, and he had worked hard and purposefully to make that idea a reality. When he accepted his current job, he had finally set foot on the path he had dreamed of, and neither the long hours nor the detailed "grunt" work that was the lot of first-year analysts gave him misgivings about his choice. He believed he was pursuing his own values by seeking a successful career at a Wall Street investment bank. It was the kind of life he wanted to live and the kind of work he enjoyed doing.

On the other hand, when Lewis considered his African-American background, he thought about what

his parents had taught him. One episode from the early
1960s stood out in particular. His parents made a reservation at a restaurant that reputedly did not serve
blacks. When they arrived, the hostess told them there
had been a mistake. The reservation was lost, and they
could not be seated. The restaurant was half empty.
Lewis's parents turned around and left. When they got
home, his mother made a new reservation under her
maiden name. (His father had been a popular local athlete, whose name was widely recognized.) The restaurant
suspected nothing. When they returned an hour later,
the hostess, though hardly overjoyed, proceeded to seat
them.

Lewis was still moved by the memory of what his parents had done, even as he sat in his office on Wall Street
many years later. With his parents' example in mind,
Lewis could begin to sense what seemed to be the best
answer to his present
dilemma. He would look
at the situation as his parents' son. He would view
it as an African-American,
not as just another young
investment banker. Lewis decided that he could not go
to the meeting as the "token black." To do so would
repudiate his parents' example. He decided, in effect,
that his race was a vital part of his moral identity, one
with a deeper and stronger relation to his core self than
the professional role he had recently assumed.

> *Self-inquiry must lead to
> shrewd, persuasive, and
> self-confident action if it is
> to be an effective tool.*

SHREWDNESS AND EXPEDIENCY

Introspection of the kind Steve Lewis engaged in can
easily become divorced from real-world demands. We

have all seen managers who unthinkingly throw themselves into a deeply felt personal cause and suffer serious personal and career setbacks. As the Renaissance philosopher Niccolò Machiavelli and other ethical pragmatists remind us, idealism untempered by realism often does little to improve the world. Hence, the next critical question becomes, *What combination of shrewdness and expediency, coupled with imagination and boldness, will help me implement my personal understanding of what is right?* This is, of course, a different question altogether from What should I do? It acknowledges that the business world is a bottom-line, rough-and-tumble arena where introspection alone won't get the job done. The process of looking inward must culminate in concrete action characterized by tenacity, persuasiveness, shrewdness, and self-confidence.

How did Lewis combine idealism with realism? He decided that he would join the presentation team, but he also gambled that he could do so on terms that were at least acceptable to him. He told the partner in charge, Bruce Anderson, that he felt honored to be asked to participate but added that he wanted to play a role in the presentation. He said he was willing to spend every minute of the next 30 hours in preparation. When Anderson asked why, Lewis said only that he wanted to earn his place on the team. Anderson reluctantly agreed. There was, it turned out, a minor element of the presentation that required the application of some basic analytical techniques with which Lewis was familiar. Lewis worked hard on the presentation, but when he stood up during the meeting for the 12 minutes allotted him, he had a terrible headache and wished he had refused Anderson's offer. His single day of cramming was no substitute for the weeks his colleagues had invested in the project. Nevertheless, his portion of the presentation went well, and he received praise from his colleagues for the work he had done.

On balance, Lewis had soundly defined the dilemma he faced and had taken an active role in solving it—he did not attend the meeting as a showpiece. At the same time, he may have strengthened his career prospects. He felt he had passed a minor test, a rite of passage at his company, and had demonstrated not only that he was willing to do what it took to get the job done but also that he would not be treated as a token member of the group. The white analysts and associates who were passed over probably grumbled a bit; but Lewis suspected that, if they had been dealt his hand, they would have played their cards as he did.

Who Are We? Defining Moments for Work Groups

As managers move up in an organization, defining moments become more difficult to resolve. In addition to looking at the situation as a conflict between two personal beliefs, managers must add another dimension: the values of their work group and their responsibilities to the people they manage. How, for example, should a manager respond to an employee who repeatedly shows up for work with the smell of alcohol on his breath? How should a manager respond to one employee who has made sexually suggestive remarks to another? In this type of defining moment, the problem and its resolution unfold not only as a personal drama within one's self but also as a drama among a group of people who work together. The issue becomes public and is important enough to define a group's future and shape its values.

POINTS OF VIEW

Many managers suffer from a kind of ethical myopia, believing that their entire group views a situation through the same lens that they do. This way of thinking rarely succeeds in bringing people together to accomplish common goals. Differences in upbringing, religion, ethnicity, and education make it difficult for any two people to view a situation similarly—let alone an entire group of people. The ethical challenge for a manager is not to impose his or her understanding of what is right on the group but to understand how other members view the dilemma. The manager must ask, *What are the other strong, persuasive interpretations of the ethics of this situation?*

A classic example of this kind of problem involved a 35-year-old manager, Peter Adario. Adario headed the marketing department of Sayer Microworld, a distributor of computer products. He was married and had three children. He had spent most of his career as a successful salesman and branch manager, and he eagerly accepted his present position because of its varied challenges. Three senior managers reporting to Adario supervised the other 50 employees in the marketing department, and Adario in turn reported to one of four vice presidents at corporate headquarters.

Adario had recently hired an account manager, Kathryn McNeil, who was a single mother. Although she was highly qualified and competent, McNeil was having a hard time keeping up with her work because of the time she needed to spend with her son. The pace at work was demanding: the company was in the middle of finishing a merger, and 60-hour work weeks had become the norm. McNeil was also having difficulty getting

along with her supervisor, Lisa Walters, a midlevel manager in the department who reported to Adario. Walters
was an ambitious, hard-driving woman who was
excelling in Sayer Microworld's fast-paced environment.
She was irritated by McNeil's chronic lateness and
unpredictable work schedule. Adario had not paid much
attention to Walters' concerns until the morning he
found a handwritten note from her on top of his pile of
unfinished paperwork. It was her second note to him in
as many weeks. Both notes complained about McNeil's
hours and requested that she be fired.

For Adario, who was himself a father and sympa-
thetic to McNeil's plight, the situation was clearly a
defining moment, pitting his belief that his employees
needed time with their families against his duty to the
department's bottom line. Adario decided to set up a
meeting. He was confident that if he sat down with the
two women the issue could somehow be resolved.
Shortly before the meeting was to begin, however,
Adario was stunned to

*Managers need to
determine if their ethical
vision will be supported
by their coworkers and
employees.*

learn that Walters had gone over his head and discussed
the issue with one of the company's senior executives.
The two then had gone to McNeil's office and had fired
her. A colleague later told him that McNeil had been
given four hours to pack her things and leave the
premises.

Where Adario saw right versus right, Walters saw
right versus wrong. She believed that the basic ethical
issue was McNeil's irresponsibility in not pulling her
weight and Adario's lack of action on the issue. McNeil's
customer account was crucial, and it was falling behind

schedule during a period of near-crisis at the company. Walters also believed that it was unfair for one member of the badly overburdened team to receive special treatment. In retrospect, Adario could see that he and Walters looked at the same facts about McNeil and reached very different conclusions. Had he recognized earlier that his view was just one interpretation among many, he might have realized that he was engaged in a difficult contest of interpretations.

INFLUENCING BEHAVIOR

Identifying competing interpretations, of course, is only part of the battle. Managers also need to take a hard look at the organization in which they work and make a realistic assessment of whose interpretation will win out in the end. A number of factors can determine which interpretation will prevail: company culture, group norms, corporate goals and company policy, and the inevitable political jockeying and battling inside organizations. In the words of the American philosopher William James, "The final victorious way of looking at things will be the most completely impressive to the normal run of minds." Therefore, managers need to ask themselves, *What point of view is most likely to win the contest of interpretations and influence the thinking and behavior of other people?*

Peter Adario would have benefited from mulling over this question. If he had done so, he might have seen the issue in terms of a larger work-family issue within the company. For Adario and McNeil, the demands of work and family meant constant fatigue, a sense of being pulled in a thousand directions, and the frustration of never catching up on all they had to do. To the other employees at Sayer Microworld, most of whom were young and not yet parents, the work-family conflict meant that they sometimes had to work longer hours because other employees had families to attend to. Given the heavy workloads they were carrying, these single employees had little sympathy for Adario's family-oriented values.

TRUTH AS PROCESS

Planning ahead is at the heart of managerial work. One needs to learn to spot problems before they blow up into crises. The same is true for defining moments in groups. They should be seen as part of a larger process that, like any other, needs to be managed. Effective managers put into place the conditions for the successful resolution of defining moments long before those moments actually present themselves. For in the words of William James, "The truth of an idea is not a stagnant property inherent in it. Truth happens to an idea. It becomes true, is made true by events. Its verity is in fact an event, a process." Managers can start creating the conditions for a particular interpretation to prevail by asking, *Have I orchestrated a process that can make my interpretation win in my group?*

Adario missed subtle signals that a process opposed to his own had been under way for some time. Recall that Walters had sent Adario two notes, each suggesting that McNeil be replaced. What were those notes actually about? Were they tentative announcements of Walters's plans or tests of Adario's authority? And what did Walters make of Adario's failure to respond? She apparently interpreted his reaction—or lack thereof—as an indication that he would not stand in the way of firing McNeil.

Walters may even have thought that Adario wanted McNeil fired but was unwilling to do it himself. In short, Adario's defining moment had gone badly because Walters presented a compelling story to the company's top management; she thereby preempted Adario and filled the vacuum that he had created through his inaction.

Instead of waiting for the issue of work versus family to arise and take the group by surprise, Adario could have anticipated the problem and taken a proactive approach to defining a work culture that valued both family and work. Adario had ample opportunity to prevent the final turn of events from occurring. He could have promoted McNeil to others inside the company. In particular, he needed to emphasize the skills and experience, especially in account management, that she brought to the company. He also could have created opportunities for people to get to know McNeil personally, even to meet her son, so that they would understand and appreciate what she was accomplishing.

PLAYING TO WIN

One of the hallmarks of a defining moment is that there is a lot at stake for all the players in the drama. More often than not, the players will put their own interests first. In this type of business setting, neither the most well-meaning intentions nor the best-designed process will get the job done. Managers must be ready to roll up their sleeves and dive into the organizational fray, putting to use appropriate and effective tactics that will make their vision a reality. They need to reflect on the question, *Am I just playing along or am I playing to win?*

At Sayer Microworld, the contest of interpretations between Walters and Adario was clearly part of a larger power struggle. If Walters didn't have her eye on Adario's job before McNeil was fired, she probably did afterward: top management seemed to like her take-charge style. Whereas Adario was lobbing underhand softball pitches, Walters was playing hardball. At Sayer Microworld, do-the-right-thing idealism without organizational savvy was the sure path to obscurity. Adario's heart was in the right place when he hired McNeil. He believed she could do the job, he admired her courage, and he wanted to create a workplace in which she could flourish. But his praiseworthy intentions needed to be backed by a knack for maneuvering, shrewdness, and political savvy. Instead, Walters seized the moment. She timed her moves carefully and found a powerful ally in the senior manager who helped her carry out her plan.

Although Adario stumbled, it is worth noting that this defining moment taught him a great deal. In following up on McNeil's firing, Adario learned through the grapevine that many other employees shared his view of the work-family dilemma, and he began acting with more confidence than he had before. He told his boss that he disagreed with the decision to fire McNeil and objected strongly to the way the decision had been made. He then told Walters that her behavior would be noted in the next performance review he put in her file. Neither Walters nor the vice president said very much in response, and the issue never came up again. Adario had staked his claim, albeit belatedly. He had learned, in the words of Machiavelli, that "a man who has no position in society cannot even get a dog to bark at him."

> *To succeed, top-level executives must negotiate their ethical vision with shareholders, customers, and employees.*

Who Is the Company? Defining Moments for Executives

Redefining the direction of one's own life and the direction of one's work group requires a thoughtful blend of personal introspection and calculated action. But the men and women charged with running entire companies sometimes face an even more complex type of defining moment. They are asked to make manifest their understanding of what is right on a large stage—one that can include labor unions, the media, shareholders, and many other company stakeholders. Consider the complexity of the dilemma faced by a CEO who has just received a report of package tampering in one of the company's over-the-counter medications. Or consider the position of an executive who needs to formulate a response to reports in the media that women and children are being treated unfairly in the company's foreign plant. These types of decisions force top-level managers to commit not just themselves or their work groups but their entire company to an irreversible course of action.

PERSONAL AND ORGANIZATIONAL STRENGTH

In the face of such overwhelming decisions, executives typically call meetings, start negotiations, and hire consultants and lawyers. Although these steps can be helpful, they can prove disappointing unless executives have taken the time, and the necessary steps, to carve out a powerful position for themselves in the debate. From a position of strength, leaders can bring forth their vision of what is right in a situation; from a position of weakness, leaders' actions are hollow and desperate. Also,

before CEOs can step forth onto society's broad stage
with a personal vision, they must make sure that their
actions will not jeopardize the well-being of their companies, the jobs of employees, and the net income of
shareholders. That means asking, *Have I done all I can to
secure my position and the strength and stability of my
organization?*

In 1988, Eduoard Sakiz, CEO of Roussel Uclaf, a
French pharmaceutical company, faced a defining
moment of this magnitude. Sakiz had to decide whether
to market the new drug RU-486, which later came to be
known as the French abortion pill. Early tests had
shown that the drug was 90% to 95% effective in induc-
ing miscarriages during the first five weeks of a woman's
pregnancy. As he considered whether to introduce the
drug, Sakiz found himself embroiled in a major international controversy. Antiabortion groups were outraged
that the drug was even under consideration. Pro-choice
groups believed the drug represented a major step forward in the battle to secure a woman's right to an abortion. Shareholders of Roussel Uclaf's parent company,
Hoechst, were for the most part opposed to RU-486's
introduction because there had been serious threats of a
major boycott against Hoechst if the drug were introduced. To the French government, also a part owner of
Roussel Uclaf, RU-486 meant a step forward in its
attempts to cut back on back-alley abortions.

There is little doubt that at one level, the decision
Sakiz faced was a personal defining moment. He was a
physician with a long-standing commitment to RU-486.
Earlier in his career while working as a medical
researcher, Sakiz had helped develop the chemical com-
pound that the drug was based on. He believed strongly
that the drug could help thousands of women, particularly those in poor countries, avoid injury or death from

botched abortions. Because he doubted that the drug would make it to market if he were not running the company, Sakiz knew he would have to secure his own position.

At another level, Sakiz had a responsibility to protect the jobs and security of his employees. He understood this to mean taking whatever steps he could to avoid painful boycotts and the risk of violence against the company. His decision was complicated by the fact that some employees were passionately committed to RU-486, whereas others opposed the drug on ethical grounds or feared that the protests and boycotts would harm Roussel Uclaf and its other products.

How could Sakiz protect his own interests and those of his employees and still introduce the drug? Whatever path he chose, he could see that he would have to assume a low public profile. It would be foolish to play the courageous lion and charge forth pronouncing the moral necessity of RU-486. There were simply too many opponents for that approach to work. It could cost him his job and drag the company through a lengthy, painful process of dangerous turmoil.

Astute executives can use defining moments as an opportunity to redefine their company's role in society.

THE ROLE OF THE ORGANIZATION IN SOCIETY

What makes this third type of defining moment so difficult is that executives are asked to form, reveal, and test not only themselves and their work groups but also their entire company and its role in society. That requires forging a plan of action that functions at three levels: the individual, the work group, and society at large. In which areas do we want to lead? In which areas do we want to follow? How should we interact with the government? With shareholders? Leaders must ask themselves, *Have I thought creatively, boldly, and imaginatively about my organization's role in society and its relationship to its stakeholders?*

What role did Sakiz want Roussel Uclaf to play? He certainly did not want to take the easy way out. Sakiz could have pleased his boss in Germany and avoided years of controversy and boycotts by withdrawing entirely from the market for contraceptives and other reproductive drugs. (Nearly all U.S. drug companies have adopted that approach.) Sakiz could have defined Roussel Uclaf's social role in standard terms—as the property of its shareholders—and argued that RU-486 had to be shelved because boycotts against Roussel Uclaf and Hoechst were likely to cost far more than the drug would earn.

Instead, Sakiz wanted to define Roussel Uclaf's role in a daring way: women seeking nonsurgical abortions and their physicians would be among the company's core stakeholders, and the company would support this constituency through astute political activism. That approach resonated with Sakiz's own core values and with what he thought the majority of employees and other stakeholders wanted. It was clear to him that he needed to find a way to introduce the drug onto the market. The only question was how.

FROM VISION TO REALITY

To make their ethical visions a reality, top-level executives must assess their opponents and allies very carefully. What allies do I have inside and outside my company? Which parties will resist or fight my efforts? Have I underestimated their power and tactical skill or overestimated their ethical commitment? Whom will I alienate with my decision? Which parties will retaliate and how? These tactical concerns can be summed up in the question, *What combination of shrewdness, creativity, and tenacity will make my vision a reality?* Machiavelli put it more succinctly: "Should I play the lion or the fox?"

Although we may never know exactly what went through Sakiz's mind, we can infer from his actions that he had no interest in playing the lion. On October 21, 1988, a month after the French government approved RU-486, Sakiz and the executive committee of Roussel Uclaf made their decision. The *New York Times* described the events in this way: "At an October 21 meeting, Sakiz surprised members of the management committee by calling for a discussion of RU-486. There, in Roussel Uclaf's ultra-modern boardroom, the pill's long-standing opponents repeated their objections: RU-486 could spark a painful boycott, it was hurting employee morale, management was devoting too much of its time to this controversy. Finally, it would never be hugely profitable because much would be sold on a cost basis to the Third World. After two hours, Sakiz again stunned the committee by calling for a vote. When he raised his own hand in favor of suspending distribution of RU-486, it was clear that the pill was doomed."

The company informed its employees of the decision on October 25. The next day, Roussel Uclaf announced publicly that it was suspending distribution of the drug because of pressure from antiabortion groups. A Roussel Uclaf official explained the decision: "The pressure groups in the United States are very powerful, maybe even more so than in France."

The company's decision and Sakiz's role in it sparked astonishment and anger. The company and its leadership, critics charged, had doomed a promising public-health tool and had set an example of cowardice. Sakiz's colleague and friend, Etienne-Emile Baluieu, whose research had been crucial to developing RU-486, called the decision "morally scandalous" and accused Sakiz of caving in to pressure. Women's groups, family-planning advocates, and physicians in the United States and Europe came down hard on Sakiz's decision. Other critics suggested sarcastically that the company's decision was no surprise because Roussel Uclaf had decided not to produce contraceptive pills in the face of controversy during the 1960s.

Three days after Roussel Uclaf announced that it would suspend distribution, the French minister of health summoned the company's vice chairman to his office and said that if the company did not resume distribution, the government would transfer the patent to another company that would. After the meeting with the minister of health, Roussel Uclaf again stunned the public: it announced the reversal of its initial decision. The company would distribute RU-486 after all.

Sakiz had achieved his goals but in a foxlike manner. He had called out to his allies and rallied them to his side, but had done so in an indirect and shrewd way. He had used the predictable responses of the many stakeholders to orchestrate a series of events that helped achieve his ends, without looking like he was leading the way. In fact, it appeared as if he were giving in to outside pressure.

Sakiz had put into place the three principal components of the third type of defining moment. First, he had secured his own future at the company. The French health ministry, which supported Sakiz, might well have been aggravated if Hoechst had appointed another CEO in Sakiz's place; it could then have retaliated against the German company in a number of ways. In addition, by having the French government participate in the decision, Sakiz was able to deflect some of the controversy about introducing the drug away from the company, protecting employees and the bottom line. Finally, Sakiz had put Roussel Uclaf in a role of technological and social leadership within French, and even international, circles.

A Bow with Great Tension

As we have moved from Steve Lewis to Peter Adario to Eduoard Sakiz, we have progressed through increasingly complex, but similar, challenges. These managers engaged in difficult acts of self-inquiry that led them to take calculated action based on their personal understanding of what was right in the given situation.

But the three met with varying degrees of success. Steve Lewis was able to balance his personal values and the realities of the business world. The result was ethically informed action that advanced his career. Peter Adario had a sound understanding of his personal values but failed to adapt them to the realities he faced in the competitive work environment at Sayer Microworld. As a result, he failed to prevent McNeil's firing and put his own career in peril. Eduoard Sakiz not only stayed

Defining moments force us to find a balance between our hearts in all their idealism and our jobs in all their messy reality.

closely connected to his personal values and those of his organization but also predicted what his opponents and allies outside the company would do. The result was the introduction of a drug that shook the world.

The nineteenth-century German philosopher Friedrich Nietzsche once wrote, "I believe it is precisely through the presence of opposites and the feelings they occasion that the great man—the bow with great tension—develops." Defining moments bring those "opposites" and "feelings" together into vivid focus. They force us to find a balance between our hearts in all their idealism and our jobs in all their messy reality. Defining moments then are not merely intellectual exercises; they are opportunities for inspired action and personal growth.

A Guide to Defining Moments

For Individuals
Who am I?

1. What feelings and intuitions are coming into conflict in this situation?
2. Which of the values that are in conflict are most deeply rooted in my life?
3. What combination of expediency and schrewdness, coupled with imagination and boldness, will help me implement my personal understanding of what is right?

For Managers of Work Groups
Who are we?

1. What are the other strong, persuasive interpretations of the ethics of this situation?

2. What point of view is most likely to win a contest of interpretations inside my organization and influence the thinking of other people?

3. Have I orchestrated a process that can make manifest the values I care about in my organization?

For Company Executives

Who is the company?

1. Have I done all I can to secure my position and the strength of my organization?

2. Have I thought creatively and boldly about my organization's role in society and its relationship to stockholders?

3. What combination of shrewdness, creativity, and tenacity will help me transform my vision into a reality?

Note

1. The names in the accounts of Steve Lewis and Peter Adario have been changed to protect the privacy of the principals involved.

Originally published in March–April 1998
Reprint 98201

This article is based on the author's latest book, Defining Moments: When Managers Must Choose between Right and Right, *published by the Harvard Business School Press in 1997.*

The Ways Chief Executive Officers Lead

CHARLES M. FARKAS AND SUZY WETLAUFER

Executive Summary

CEOS INSPIRE SENTIMENTS FROM AWE TO WRATH, but there is little debate over their importance in the business world. Their decisions change companies and lives. But what do CEOs do all day? Where do they go? Charles Farkas and Suzy Wetlaufer analyzed interviews with 160 chief executives around the world and examined the attitudes, activities, and behaviors that shape the answers to these questions. At the outset, the authors thought they might find 160 approaches to leadership. Instead, they identified only 5, each with a singular focus: strategy, people, expertise, controls, or change.

No matter what a company makes or where it is located, its CEO must develop a philosophy about how he or she can best add value. This philosophy determines the CEO's approach to leadership. For instance, Al Zeien, CEO of Gillette, is a classic human-assets leader: He personally conducts 800 performance reviews per year. Richard Rosenberg, chairman of BankAmerica, is a typical box leader: He spends the bulk of his time designing strict controls to help his company navigate in a highly regulated environment.

Is a CEO's leadership approach simply a matter of personal style? Not necessarily. The authors found that the most successful companies, CEOs adopt the approach that will meet the needs of the organization and the business situation at hand. Sometimes the approach fits the CEO's personality; sometimes it does not. The authors also found that some CEOs fail to employ a consistent approach to leadership. That is a mistake. The stakes are too high for a CEO to lead without the commitment and clarity that one of the five approaches can provide.

THERE IS NO SHORTAGE OF SCHOOLS FOR BUSI-NESS-PEOPLE of every specialty: accountants, engineers, financiers, technologists, information specialists, marketers, and, of course, general managers, who have their choice of hundreds, if not thousands, of M.B.A. programs. But where is the school for the person in charge of getting the best results from all these members of the organization? There is no school for CEOs—except the school of experience. Chief executives must learn on the job how to lead a company, and they must learn while every stakeholder is watching.

CEOs must learn on the job, and they must learn while every stakeholder is watching.

The CEO's job is like no other in the organization. It is infinite. Senior executives are, by definition, ultimately responsible for every decision and action of every member of the company, including those decisions and actions of which they are not aware. CEOs—even new ones—are allowed few mistakes. Not surprisingly, research shows that between 35% and 50% of all CEOs are replaced within five years. That is a costly proposition for any organization, for no company can lose its leader without losing some sense, even temporarily, of its identity and direction.

Two years ago, our interest in the role of the CEO prompted us to begin an extensive study of how senior executives lead. Over 12 months, we interviewed 160 chief executives around the world, most of whom were running major corporations in industries as diverse as gold mining, computers, and soft drinks. Our goal was to examine the set of attitudes, activities, and behaviors that determined how those executives managed their organizations. To be honest, going into the project we hypothesized that there might turn out to be 160 different approaches to leadership. There were not. Only 5 distinct approaches emerged from our data.

No matter where a company is located or what it makes, its CEO must develop a guiding, overarching philosophy about how he or she can best add value. This philosophy determines the CEO's approach to leadership. By *approach,* we mean which areas of corporate policy—for example, strategic planning, R&D, or recruiting—receive the most attention, what kind of people and behaviors the CEO values in the organization, which decisions the CEO makes personally or delegates, and how he or she spends each day. A leadership approach is a coherent, explicit style of management, not a reflection of personal style. This is a critical distinction. (See "What's Personality Got to Do with It?" on page 243) We found that in effective companies, CEOs do not simply adopt the leadership approach that suits their personalities but instead adopt the approach that will best meet the needs of the organization and the business situation at hand. Is the industry growing explosively or is it mature? How many competitors exist and how strong are they? Does technology matter and, if so, where is it going? What are the organization's capital and human assets? What constitutes sustainable competitive advantage, and how close is the organization to achieving it? The answers to questions such as these determine which of the following five leadership approaches an effective CEO will adopt.

1. The strategy approach. CEOs who use this approach believe that their most important job is to create, test, and design the implementation of long-term strategy, extending in some cases into the distant future. Their position overseeing all areas of the corporation, they explain, gives them the unique ability to determine their organizations' allocation of resources and optimal direction. On a day-to-day basis, they spend their time in activities intended to ascertain their organizations' point of departure (the current business situation) and point of arrival (the most advantageous market position in the future). These CEOs devote approximately 80% of their time to matters external to the organization's operations—customers, competitors, technological advances, and market trends—as opposed to internal matters such as hiring or control systems. It follows, then, that they tend to value employees to whom they can delegate the day-to-day operation of their organizations as well as those who possess finely tuned analytical and planning skills.

2. The human-assets approach. In marked contrast to CEOs in the above group, human-assets CEOs strongly believe that strategy formulation belongs close to the markets, in the business units. According to these CEOs, their primary job is to impart to their organizations certain values, behaviors, and attitudes by closely managing the growth and development of individuals. These executives travel constantly, spending the majority of their time in personnel-related activities such as recruiting, performance reviews, and career mapping. Their goal is to create a universe of satellite CEOs: people at every level of the organization who act and make decisions as the CEO would. Not surprisingly, these executives value long-term employees who consistently exhibit "company way" behaviors, as opposed to so-called mavericks, who do not always adhere to organizational norms.

3. The expertise approach. Executives who lead by using this approach believe that the CEO's most important responsibility is selecting and disseminating within the corporation an area of expertise that will be a source of competitive advantage. Their schedules show that they devote the majority of their time to activities related to the cultivation and continual improvement of the expertise, such as studying new technological research, analyzing competitors' products, and meeting with engineers and customers. They often focus on designing programs, systems, and procedures, such as promotion policies and training plans, that reward people who acquire the expertise and share it across the borders of business units and functions. These CEOs tend to hire people who are trained in the expertise, but they also seek candidates who possess flexible minds, lack biases, and demonstrate a willingness to be immersed—*indoctrinated* is not too strong a word—in the expertise.

4. The box approach. CEOs in this category believe that they can add the most value in their organizations by creating, communicating, and monitoring an explicit set of controls—financial, cultural, or both—that ensure uniform, predictable behaviors and experiences for customers and employees. CEOs who use this approach believe that their companies' success depends on the ability to provide customers with a consistent and risk-free experience. As a result, these executives spend their days attending to exceptions to their organizations' controls, such as quarterly results that are below expectations or a project that misses its deadline. In addition, they devote more time than the other types of CEOs to developing detailed, prescriptive policies, procedures, and rewards to reinforce desired behaviors. Finally, these executives tend to value seniority within the organization, often promoting people with many years of service to the corporate team and rarely hiring top-level executives from outside the company.

5. The change approach. Executives in this category are guided by the belief that the CEO's most critical role is to create an environment of continual reinvention, even if such an environment produces anxiety and confusion, leads to some strategic mistakes, and temporarily hurts financial performance. In contrast to CEOs who employ the strategy approach, these CEOs focus not on a specific point of arrival for their organizations but on the process of getting there. Similarly, their focus contrasts starkly with that of a box leader: Control systems, written reports, planning cycles, policies, and rules do not seem to interest these so-called change agents. Instead, they spend as much as 75% of their time using speeches, meetings, and other forms of communication to motivate members of their organizations to embrace the gestalt of change. They spend their days in the field, meeting with a wide range of stakeholders, from customers to investors to suppliers to employees at virtually all levels of the organization. Not surprisingly, the people they value are usually those who could be called aggressive and independent—people who view their jobs not as entitlements but as opportunities for advancement that must be seized every day. Seniority matters little to the change agent; passion, energy, and an openness to a new, reinvented tomorrow matter much more.

In the following pages, we will describe the five leadership approaches in more detail and explore which business situations call for which approaches. There is, naturally, some overlap. CEOs who adopt the strategy approach might use elements of human-assets leadership, for example. Some box CEOs employ the techniques of a strategy leader to address the out-of-the-box issues that can be overlooked in control-oriented organizations. That said, however, our research suggests that in most effectively run organizations, CEOs select a dominant approach, using it as the compass and rudder that direct all corporate decisions and actions. Our research also suggests that a CEO's approach can and should change over the course of his or her tenure. As one of our subjects, Edzard Reuter, CEO of automaker Daimler-Benz, says, "A business is a living organism.

There will always be a point where the environment changes, the competition changes, something critical changes, and you must realize this and take the leading role in meeting change."

Whatever the approach, then, the CEO's role is to act decisively and boldly—a demand of high-level leadership taught only by on-the-job training.

The Strategy Approach: Focusing on the Future, Near and Far

Of all the hypotheses we held at the start of our research, none felt as unassailable as our supposition that the vast majority of CEOs consider themselves the corporation's chief visionary, responsible for setting short- and long-term strategy. Our data told another story: Of the 160 executives we interviewed, less than 20% subscribed to that leadership approach. In fact, the prevailing opinion of our subjects was that those with the most frequent and meaningful contact with customers and competitors should be responsible for strategic assessment and planning. Peter George, chief executive of Ladbroke Group, a British gaming and hotel concern, puts it simply: "Strategy is the domain of the business units because the people running them are closest to the markets."

Open a strategy CEO's schedule book and you'll see time devoted to collecting, cultivating, and analyzing vast amounts of data.

Nevertheless, we did encounter a distinct group of CEOs guided by the belief that their position gives them the best vantage point for making decisions about capital allocations, resource management, investments in technology, new products, and locations for doing business. For this reason, they assert, the CEO alone (although often supported by a small corporate team) is equipped to determine exactly where the company in all its parts and units should go, and how fast.

Open a strategy CEO's schedule book. What you will see is time allotted with a common theme: the collection, cultivation, and analysis of data. These CEOs devote much of their days to the activities that ultimately yield strategic decisions. They rigorously gather and test information about markets, economic trends, customers' purchasing patterns, competitors' capabilities, and other matters external to their organizations' operations. To increase their sources of data, these executives frequently use company task forces or outside consultants and eagerly draw on other sources of information and opinion, such as fundamental research, trade publications, and independent surveys. Strategy CEOs strive to understand how their customers behave and what really matters to them. They also seek to know as much as possible about every competitor's strengths, technologies, and key customer segments. Moreover, a strategy CEO focuses on knowing the organization's capabilities, or how well the organization can deliver on its strategy. What can the company do? What can't it do? What are its lowest costs, highest quality, and fastest speed of delivery? In sum, strategy leaders devote themselves to understanding the company's point of departure, selecting its point of arrival, and, perhaps most important, mapping the route between them.

How do they achieve all that? More than executives in any other category, strategy CEOs employ extensive analysis as well as reporting and planning systems that test strategic scenarios, and they often focus the work of their corporate teams around these systems. For example, Coca-Cola's CEO, Roberto Goizueta, oversees a program in which country managers spend three days every six months in planning sessions with the top corporate team, examining every aspect of their businesses. "We debate what we are doing right, what is working, and what we are doing wrong," says John Hunter, principal operating officer and executive vice president for the company's international operations. "We talk about strategies for the next year and the next three years. We ask, 'What's going to change in terms of our consumer, our market, the marketplace environment, the competitors, and our bottler system?' We run down and review all these things, and then we say, 'Where do we need to be three years from now and what do we need to do to get there?'" Several weeks after these meetings, the country managers fly to Coke's headquarters in Atlanta, Georgia, to present their one- and three-year strategic plans and operating budgets in another demanding process of debate, testing, and planning. As is the case at many companies led by strategy CEOs, these kinds of sessions are supplemented by several other forums throughout the year devoted to strategy analysis and formulation.

Michael Dell of Dell Computer is another CEO who plots his company's short- and long-term strategic path by gathering vast amounts of data. The company, which assembles personal computers, has specially trained employees who take 50,000 phone calls from customers every day and document and organize their comments, which are then distributed to managers. In addition, every Friday, Dell managers from every functional area in every plant and office around the world gather in customer-advocate meetings, in which a dissatisfied customer addresses the managers over a speakerphone.

"The point is to sensitize the entire organization to the customer," Dell explains. "We want to make everyone literally hear the voice of the customer, to hear the frustration when we do something that makes it difficult to use our products." Phone calls from customers are also used to spark ideas for new products and services. As a result of many calls from people wondering if Dell made a small, powerful notebook computer, for example, the company began assembling and distributing a 100-megahertz Pentium-chip model. Dell was among the first to market with the product. Michael Dell himself also logs on to the Internet on a daily basis, scanning the bulletin boards and chat rooms used most frequently by industry insiders and computer devotees for information and opinions about market trends and for reactions to his company's—and his competitors'—products.

What makes a CEO decide to take on the role of chief strategist? Our research indicates that neither industry type nor a company's national origin seems to be a determining factor. Instead, one relevant issue appears to be the level of complexity in the company or industry, in terms of technology, geography, or organizational structure. Coca-Cola, for example, has 32,000 employees in nearly 200 countries around the world. The volume and pace of change seem particularly relevant as well. The less stable the situation, the more likely the CEO is to believe that he or she must be both lookout and navigator. To play those roles well, we heard, the CEO needs all the data-driven insight that this approach to leadership generates. Finally, we found that the strategy approach

Some companies are too complex or too straightforward to make long-term planning a wise use of the CEO's time.

is often selected by CEOs who must frequently make decisions that have enormous consequences. Again, this approach provides the kind of information and involves the sort of testing and planning that well-calculated risk taking requires.

The Human-Assets Approach: Managing One Person at a Time

Not every CEO who adopts the human-assets approach thinks that strategy belongs in the business units, but most do. Their companies, many of the CEOs in this category explain, are either too complex or, interestingly, too straightforward to make long-term strategic planning a wise use of the CEO's time. Instead, these executives believe that in their particular organizations, success depends on superior execution—the way members of their companies make decisions, interact with customers, roll out new products, or design programs to deflect or defeat the competition. Accordingly, they believe that their imperative is to hire and cultivate the kind of individuals who will act intelligently, swiftly, and appropriately without direct or constant supervision. And they believe the way to develop such individuals is by shaping the values and behaviors of virtually every member of the organization into "company way" values and behaviors through a coherent set of systems, programs, and policies. Our research indicates that this approach to leadership is the second most prevalent after the box approach and is employed by about 22% of the CEOs we surveyed.

As a group, human-assets CEOs communicate and demonstrate what they want face-to-face. Their travel schedules rival that of a secretary of state or foreign minister, with as much as 90% of their time spent out of the office. "People have asked me time and again, 'Why do you spend all that time traveling?' And the answer to that is really kind of simple," says Al Zeien, CEO of Gillette, the personal-care-products company with 34,000 employees worldwide. "I travel because that's where the people are. I travel because I want to be sure that people who are making the decisions in, say, Argentina have the same reference base as I do for the company. I want to make sure they are all using the same ground rules I would use. I want to see if they have the same objectives. I travel because you can only find these kinds of things on the home ground."

While they are traveling, human-assets CEOs tend to focus on several specific aspects of corporate policy. The first of these is hiring, an area that occupies human-assets CEOs more than it does chief executives in any other category. At PepsiCo, for example, CEO Wayne Calloway interviews every candidate for the top 600 jobs in the company. "It doesn't matter if they're going to work in Pakistan or Philadelphia—I get to talk to them," he says. "We have the chance to get to know each other and make sure we have the same values and objectives and standards in mind. That way, when they're back in Pakistan and somebody wants to do something, they will say, 'Well, I don't know. That's not what I heard, and I heard it straight from Calloway himself, so I think that's not what we ought to be doing.'" Calloway, like many other human-assets CEOs, also occasionally monitors hiring at lower levels of the organization. For example, he was once involved in hiring two new M.B.A.'s into PepsiCo's office in Wichita, Kansas. Similarly, Herb Kelleher of Southwest Airlines says that he has participated in the selection of ramp agents at small regional airports. Hiring, he explains, is "where it starts. It's the head of the river, and if you pollute that, then you gradually pollute everything downstream." Speaking more generally of his approach to leadership, Kelleher sounds another theme of human-assets CEOs: "We hire great attitudes, and we'll teach them any functionality that they need."

Human-assets CEOs also focus on other areas of personnel management, such as training, incentives, career planning, and programs to increase retention. Al Zeien, for instance, personally conducts 800 performance reviews per year at Gillette, monitoring employees for their commitment to acting in ways that benefit the entire company, not just their units or countries. He attends product development meetings in virtually every division of the company to monitor R&D efforts, of course, but also to identify star employees whom he can point in directions they might not otherwise go. He once, for example, engineered the move of a manager from New Zealand to Gillette's operations in Redwood City, California, because he thought that the manager showed great promise and that the transfer would benefit the man's career and the company. The New Zealander's boss had told Zeien that the man would never leave his native country, so Zeien did what any human-assets CEO would do: He flew to New Zealand to convince the employee in person. The man accepted the appointment.

Other human-assets CEOs show the same kind of attention to personnel matters. At the British food manufacturer United Biscuits, for example, chief executive Eric Nicoli oversees a system that evaluates the performance of hundreds of employees semiannually.

The goal is to ensure that "motivated, caring, and optimistic" members of the organization are identified and rewarded, and that others are retrained or let go. Echoing many other CEOs in this category, Nicoli notes that close attention to so many individuals and careers requires an enormous commitment of time but that it is the only way to manage an operation in which the CEO simply cannot be everywhere or know everything.

Although most human-assets CEOs tend to value employees who display predictable "company way" values such as honesty and loyalty to the corporation, they also believe in individual empowerment. These CEOs can and do give authority to members of the organization to act quickly and freely, without corporate approval. This authority to act is awarded only to employees who already conform to the company's way of doing things. But in organizations led by effective human-assets CEOs, this group of proven team players is often large. Consider what happened at Southwest Airlines when Midway Airlines went out of business in 1991. Within hours of Midway's announcement, Southwest employees from Dallas had physically taken over every Midway gate at the Chicago airport. "I didn't even know they were going to Chicago when they left. They didn't call me first," Kelleher recalls. "They came in later and said, 'Hey, Chief, we just did something; we thought you might like to know about it.'" They never doubted his approval, Kelleher notes, because "we have such a great congruency among our people." Congruency of values, and of the actions born from them in the daily execution of corporate strategy, is the essence of the human-assets approach.

The Expertise Approach: Championing Knowledge

A small but distinct portion of the CEOs we interviewed, less than 15%, say that their main role is to select, cultivate, and spread a competitive expertise up, down, and across the business units of the organization. Put another way, these chief executives believe that they must create a specific capability that will allow the organization to differentiate itself from its competitors and will thereby lead the company to a position of sustainable advantage. Expertise, we found, can be a process. Julian Ogilvie Thompson, chairman of the South African mining company Anglo American, devotes the bulk of his time to honing and disseminating within the organization the company's unique competence in deep-mining technologies. Expertise can be a package of ideas and techniques, such as the focus on the brand-consumer relationship that drives the leadership of Charlotte Beers, CEO of the international advertising agency Ogilvy & Mather. Expertise can also be a concept. At Motorola, the CEO's commitment to unassailable quality defines the work of the corporate office. When does a CEO decide to use the expertise approach? When he or she believes that a well-conceived, carefully developed area of competence is the surest way to gain and sustain a competitive advantage.

CEOs who use the expertise approach don't just preach the gospel of their expertise; they create programs to reinforce it.

In their daily activities, expertise CEOs cover more organizational territory than CEOs from any other category because they do not become as involved in operational details. Instead, they focus on shaping corporate policies that will strengthen their organizations' competencies. In hiring, for example, expertise CEOs do not generally conduct interviews. They do, however, design and monitor the policies behind the hiring process to ensure that their companies will attract candidates who are experienced in the area of expertise or who seem inclined to become fully immersed in it. Similarly, expertise CEOs make sure that their companies' incentive programs reward employees who cultivate the expertise and share it with colleagues. And they design control and reporting systems that track their companies' missions and establish a focal point for all activity in the corporation. Expertise CEOs usually do not devote much time to gathering or analyzing data. But they direct those who perform that work to collect data that will help them determine which types of knowledge or competencies are relevant to consumers, which competitors have the edge, and how much it will cost to be the best.

An expertise CEO spends much of his or her time focusing the organization on its area of expertise and sending strong messages about the company's priorities. At Motorola, for example, former CEO Robert Galvin would walk out of meetings about a business unit's performance after quality figures were discussed, vividly demonstrating what he deemed the company's unique competence and his number one concern. CEOs who lead in this way, however, don't just preach the gospel of their selected expertise; they are proficient at creating programs or systems that reinforce it. At Houston-based Cooper Industries, which specializes in basic low-tech manufacturing, CEO Robert Cizik deploys "SWAT teams" of manufacturing experts from within the company that travel from division to division to investigate and upgrade factory-floor practices and equipment. The teams have clout: Their reports go directly to the CEO's office, and a yearlong stint on one of these teams is mandatory for managers who want to move up in the organization. At Anglo American, Ogilvie Thompson has developed a cadre of highly skilled men and women, called "consulting engineers," who travel to the company's operations around the world and serve as line managers wherever they go. The consulting engineers, he says, "pick up an idea from the chaps at Premier diamond mine, who are running the operations with skill, and are able to transfer this idea to the DeBeers group mines in Namibia or Botswana, really for free, adding value to others." Ogilvie Thompson's commitment to this group—he often personally decides who becomes a consulting engineer and determines where each will be assigned—reflects his commitment to the company's expertise.

Expertise CEOs formed the smallest group that emerged in our research. The reason, we believe, lies in the difficulty of sustaining the approach. With the free flow of information and people between companies and countries, expertise is hard to keep proprietary. In addition, an expertise won't remain relevant for long in an ever changing marketplace. Virtually every CEO in this category acknowledges these challenges. Cooper's Robert Cizik believes that his company will soon need to embrace a new competence to stay ahead. And Charlotte Beers notes that competitors can and do "borrow" the marketing techniques Ogilvy & Mather pioneered, the *brand print* and *brand probe.* But like many proponents of this approach, Beers advocates expertise leadership for focusing an organization on what it must do to compete and win.

The Box Approach: Applying the Pressure of Orthodoxy

From the most entrepreneurial software company to the most conservative bank, every company has a *box*—a set of procedural, financial, and cultural controls to which members of the organization must conform. All CEOs spend some of their time designing and maintaining controls, and evaluating the performance of business units and employees relative to those controls. But CEOs who are truly box leaders view these tasks as their primary responsibility. Our research shows that CEOs using this approach are often running companies in highly regulated industries, such as banking, or in industries in which safety is a paramount concern, such as airlines. These executives explain that their business situations allow virtually no margin for error, a reality that turns the design and application of strict controls into the CEO's highest priority.

Box CEOs often sound remarkably similar to human-assets executives. Leaders from both categories say that they are trying to build organizations in which each individual, in any circumstance, will act just as the CEO would. But instead of using personnel development and the inculcation of values as their means, box CEOs use control systems. Many of these executives say that "building frameworks" and "drawing boundaries" are their primary responsibilities. In other words, they create explicit rules and rewards for acceptable behaviors, outcomes, and results. With such controls in place, box CEOs

All CEOs spend some of their time designing and maintaining controls, but true box leaders see this as their main responsibility.

spend much of their time attending to the exceptions—
tracking down the reasons for missed deadlines, unexpected losses, or below-average performances of divisions or employees. These CEOs frequently use internal
reviews and external audits, employee rating scales,
strict policies, and financial reports. They usually spend
their days at corporate headquarters meeting with the
managers responsible for business units or with other
members of the corporate team, and scrutinizing proposals for new programs or requests for resource allocations. They study reports from the field concerning
performance, often request additional data, and rigorously question what they see and hear. Finally, box CEOs
tend to be intensely involved in company communications, both external and internal. Maurice Lippens, chairman of Fortis, an international financial-services company based in Belgium, puts an umbrella over all these
activities when he describes his most important role as
"applying the pressure of orthodoxy to the corporation."
This phrase captures the essence of the box CEO.

Thirty percent of the CEOs we interviewed devote
enough of their time and attention to the techniques
mentioned above to be considered box leaders. Lippens,
for example, employs
hundreds of auditors to
monitor the perform-
ance of each business
unit on an ongoing basis
and benchmark it
against other units as
well as competitors. At HSBC Holdings, formerly known
as HongKong Shanghai Banking Company, chief executive John Bond oversees guidelines that control every
aspect of the company's information technology system.

*Control systems can be
stifling, but they bring
clarity and predictability—
two powerful competitive
forces.*

The small staff of experts who run the bank's computer network are located at headquarters in London and are charged with maintaining a system that cannot "be tinkered with," in Bond's words. Moreover, Bond carefully monitors other aspects of the bank's information systems. "Every unit writes a technology plan each year on what they plan to spend on development, what they plan to spend on operations, and what equipment they plan to buy," he says. "That is reviewed here down to the last PC, and we will say, 'You don't need to buy a new computer in Malaysia; we can supply it from Indonesia.' We can control the movement of equipment around the world from London, and I can assure you it is a very detailed plan, but it isn't very popular."

Bond is not the only box CEO who acknowledges the negative side effects of the approach. Control systems can be stifling for those at the receiving end. But he also notes, like many other executives in this category, that the box approach brings enormous clarity and predictability, both of which can be powerful competitive weapons.

The president of AXA has invented a special language to unify 50,000 employees.

"We believe ours is a business based on trust," Bond says of HSBC Holdings, which operates 3,000 banking offices in 68 countries. The company's control system leads to consistent performance by tellers and credit officers branch to branch, country to country, year to year. Such consistency begets trust. "The customers love it," Bond says.

The box approach is most prevalent in industries that demand strict procedural and financial controls, but we also found some CEOs using controls that were more cultural in nature. One example is Claude Bébéar, president of AXA Group, an international insurance company based in France. Bébéar has invented a language of words and symbols in an effort to create uniform priorities, behaviors, and goals among the organization's 50,000 employees in 12 countries. The language includes phrases such as "TNT action" and "the trap of immobility." Employees across units and national borders are encouraged to use the first phrase to express the rapid implementation of decisions and the second to describe where people find themselves when they are unwilling to change. The point of the shared language, Bébéar says, is to create a corps of like-minded employees who freely and clearly exchange intelligence and technical advice, both of which are competitive weapons in the decentralized insurance and financial services markets. Called AXAnetics, the company's language is taught annually to thousands of employees in a French castle recently converted into the company's university.

Despite their attention to control systems, almost all box CEOs devote some time to cultivating, in small doses, the kind of creative, nonconformist behavior that their approach usually does not reward. At BankAmerica, for instance, chairman Richard Rosenberg reads dozens of internal newsletters in search of fresh and innovative marketing ideas—and thinkers—to introduce to the rest of the organization. At NatWest Group, one of the United Kingdom's largest banks, chief executive Derek Wanless leads several teams of employees in an effort to draw individuals out of their highly structured roles and to encourage them to bring their creativity to issues such as diversity and new products and services. And at British Airways, chairman Colin Marshall regularly travels to airports and BA offices to meet with small groups of employees for sessions of what he calls "listening to the moaning." Marshall admits that he sometimes hears complaints about the company's degree of centralized authority. But he is quick to point out that, for the most part, people at BA do in fact understand the purpose of the organization's tight controls. Speaking for many CEOs in this category, he asserts that of all the leadership approaches, the box approach is the best way to deliver what the customer wants most: no surprises.

The Change Approach: Upending the Status Quo

It's hard to be a CEO today without talking about the importance of change. With all the positive press change gets, virtually every constituent group, from shareholders to employees, expects to hear that change is under way or at least planned for the near future. Indeed, the majority of CEOs in our study, even those who use the box approach, talk about initiating, championing, or simply overseeing change. But a much smaller group, about 15% of the total, actually fall into the category of change agents. These CEOs identify their chief role as directing the complete overhaul of practically everything about their companies, down to the fundamental underpinnings.

Unlike strategy CEOs, change agents focus not on where their organizations will end up but on how they will get there.

Unlike strategy CEOs, change agents focus not on where their organizations will end up but on how they will get there. These CEOs cultivate an environment of constant questioning and risk taking, and frequent reinvention of business practices and products. Change, these CEOs explain, is the best way to deliver consistently extraordinary results. It should be noted that the CEOs we identified as change agents are all leading profitable organizations. But they still believe that deeply entrenched ways of doing business will ultimately be their companies' undoing. Their job, as they see it, is to create an environment of constant renewal. Indeed, a leitmotiv of our conversations with these chief executives was their goal of building not just better organizations but organizations that enthusiastically embrace ambiguity, uncertainty, and upheaval.

Compared with CEOs in other categories, change agents are rather unconcerned with financial or procedural controls, written reports, planning cycles, and guidelines. They spend their days meeting with employees, customers, suppliers, and shareholders to champion change and encourage others to do the same—or at least to be patient while change is under way. Virtually no one is neglected. Change agents visit factories to talk with line workers, attend company picnics, and answer their E-mail and voice mail messages daily.

All areas of corporate policy do, in relatively even doses, receive the change agent's attention. But if any area receives special attention, it is compensation, perhaps because pay and promotion are two of the most powerful tools for overcoming the aversion many people have to what is new and unpredictable. The first official act of many change agents, in fact, is to revamp their companies' performance-review and reward systems. Managers responsible for recruiting, for example, are instructed to hire nonconformists and risk takers, and then receive bonuses for doing so. Engineers or scientists in R&D are compensated for breakthrough products rather than product extensions. Stephen Friedman, the former managing partner of the investment bank Goldman Sachs, relates an example of how his organization realigned rewards to promote change. When the bank's leadership team initially decided that the organization had to expand internationally to stay competitive, there were few volunteers for its foreign offices. "It was just not valued as an attractive career opportunity by most of our U.S. people, and their spouses didn't necessarily want to go, and their dogs couldn't possibly endure living in Tokyo," Friedman recalls. "So we took an exceptionally talented young banker and promoted him to partner two years ahead of his class because he went to Asia at great personal sacrifice."

Friedman recounts another experience that illustrates one of the change agent's most important techniques: consensus building. Because change can be extremely disconcerting to members of an organization, change agents must often shepherd new ideas over rough terrain. For example, one of Friedman's first steps as a change agent in the early 1980s was to form a strategic planning committee in the investment banking division. "We composed the committee of bright, iconoclastic, younger people below the senior managerial levels, so they had no compulsion to defend the status quo," he says. Several members of this committee suggested that Goldman get into the junk bond business. Friedman came to support the idea, but he knew that his personal enthusiasm wouldn't carry the day within the bank, long a bastion of conservatism. For help, Friedman asked an experienced partner, widely considered to be among the bank's most intelligent and cautious, to conduct a study to determine whether and how Goldman should enter the junk bond business. "He came to the same conclusion we did, but with a lot more documentation and some useful refinements," Friedman says. "And now he had bought in and was behind the plan. It had establishment blessing."

Change agents often combine consensus building with another, somewhat contradictory technique: occasional public and dramatic displays of top management's strong support for new ways of doing business. At Tenneco, CEO Dana Mead sets virtually unattainable financial targets for the business units and then actually incorporates them into the budget. He requires Tenneco's five divisional CEOs to give monthly presentations about their performance relative to those targets in an open forum. "The pressure this builds is terrific, and it works," he notes. Mead, like many other executives in this category, relies heavily on company newsletters to communicate, and many change agents create monthly or quarterly videos that extol areas of their companies that have come up with innovative products or programs. CEOs in this category also communicate through their actions, firing high-profile managers who are not effecting change quickly enough, or divesting entire divisions for the same reason. J. P. Bolduc, the former CEO of W.R. Grace, recalls that he sold a Belgian mattress-ticking manufacturer that was one of the company's best-performing subsidiaries because it didn't fit into his new, "reinvented" vision of the company. The move, he says, put W.R. Grace in "cultural shock." But, he adds, "nobody believed what we were trying to do, so it became clear we had to break through the sound barrier." This kind of move appears to be the flip side of the change agent's use of consensus building, but the two form sum and substance of the approach.

Finally, change agents are distinct in their enthusiasm for the kinds of individuals who are often unwel-
come in other types of organizations. These CEOs tend
to value, as Dana Mead puts it, "recalcitrants, trouble-
makers, or gadflies." Mead admits that such people don't
always make for smooth meetings, but they do raise the
kinds of questions and launch the kinds of plans that
lead to substantial change. As an example, Mead points
to an employee he hired soon after his appointment as
CEO. The man had come to the United States as a
refugee, worked his way through Stanford University,
and then went on to become a White House Fellow. "He
is the most aggressive, smartest guy you have ever seen,
but he can stir things up and step on toes," Mead says,
noting that he has had to placate the man's direct bosses
more than once. But, he adds, "he is exactly the mold we
would like to see around here. He brings in some very
exciting projects for us, and he delivers results."

Not surprisingly, our research suggests that a CEO
who takes on the role of change agent takes on perhaps
the most demanding and daunting of the five leadership
approaches. Change is almost always accompanied by
controversy, discomfort, and resistance. All the change
agents in our survey comment on this frustrating reality.
They also describe how this approach often forces them
to rise above their natural inclinations to move more
slowly or give people more leeway. That is, the change
approach sometimes requires people to lead in ways
inconsistent with their personalities. But Stephen Friedman speaks for many change agents when he describes
the approach as more of a calling than a management
style. "Change for the sake of change makes no sense,
of course," he says. "But if you're not working for

constructive strategic change, then you are the steward of something that *must,* by definition, erode. Competitors will surpass you, and clients will find you less relevant. If that was your approach, why would you even want the job?"

A Framework for Understanding Leadership

During a recent forum on business in the year 2001, we were asked if we had concluded from our research that, in fact, CEOs were becoming obsolete. With business units in so many companies independently making decisions that used to be the sole right of the corporate office, the questioning went, what was really left for the CEO to do all day? How could he or she continue to add value?

Our immediate answer was that CEOs do play a relevant role in business. That role is leadership, but not leadership defined as an outgrowth of a strong and charismatic personality—a talent born and not made. Some people are naturally given to inspiring the troops and leading charges, but business leaders must also *The stakes are too high for a CEO to lead without clarity, consistency, and commitment.* create a clear purpose and direction for an organization. And they must align all corporate systems with that direction for a sustained period and build organizational commitment to common goals. The five approaches that emerged from our research are the five ways that many CEOs choose to deliver clarity, consistency, and commitment.

In the course of our research, we encountered thriving organizations and those in severe crisis. What role does the CEO's approach to leadership play? Does a well-planned approach correctly matched to the business situation yield success? We are still analyzing that fundamental issue. A strong link appears to exist, but we cannot yet demonstrate a direct correlation.

What we can state definitively from our research thus far is not exactly what we set out to find. We have found that some CEOs simply do not lead, try as they might. Some employ a little of each of the five leadership approaches simultaneously, destroying organizational focus and thus organizational effectiveness. For some, their days are driven by whatever event appears on their calendars or whatever crises erupt. Others act according to their natural inclinations, doing what feels enjoyable and easy. At best, those ways of leading create confusion; at worst, they create misguided or unguided organizations. Either way, they are a mistake. The stakes are too high for a chief executive to lead without conscious intent.

The five approaches that emerged from our research are certainly not boilerplate solutions for success, nor are they rigid roles in which all CEOs can be cast. Business is too complex for such simple analysis. But the five approaches do offer a framework for understanding how CEOs manage to give structure and meaning to their infinite jobs, learning to lead as they go.

What's Personality Got to Do with It?

"BUT ISN'T LEADERSHIP REALLY ALL ABOUT PERSONALITY?" We hear this question frequently during discussions about our research and the five leadership approaches. We also often hear this remark: "Leadership—either you're born with it or you're not."

We disagree, both that leadership is a genetic trait and that a person's approach to leadership is solely a function of personality. In fact, we found that personality is just one element of effective leadership and often not the decisive one. In the most successful companies, the CEO has scrutinized the business situation, determined what the organization requires from its leader, and chosen the leadership approach that best meets those requirements. Sometimes the approach fits the CEO's personality; sometimes it does not. Indeed, our research suggests that some very good leaders repress certain personality traits, or develop ones they weren't born with, in order to run their organizations effectively.

Consider Richard Rosenberg of BankAmerica. He employs, by his own admission and our observation, the box approach to leadership. He says that he must: BankAmerica operates in a highly regulated industry. A small error or, worse, a case of graft can have grave consequences. BankAmerica thus owes it to its customers to have a strict set of controls, and the CEO must make them his chief responsibility.

But is Richard Rosenberg the kind of person you would expect to be using the box approach? Hardly. He is relaxed, affable, gregarious. "This isn't me," he admits. "I'm not a box guy. I'd actually fit in a lot better with the people in marketing. But our situation demanded a box. So here I am."

And take a look at Dana Mead, CEO of Tenneco. When Mead was appointed to lead the $3 billion diversified industrial concern in early 1992, he thought that the company was headed in the right direction. Instead, he quickly discovered that Tenneco was entirely off course. The company had some attractive businesses, but many of its practices prevented those businesses from thriving. There was a highly politicized capital-allocation system, a compensation program that measured and rewarded meaningless goals, and no strategy formulation process. Without a complete overhaul, Mead determined, the company would not survive into the next century. The battle plan: change. Accordingly, Mead adopted practically every technique of the change approach to leadership. He launched new policies and procedures, established a new culture, divested operations, fired employees unwilling or unable to embrace new ways of doing business, and went on the road to preach the gospel of change to Tenneco employees all over the world.

But does Mead have the kind of personality you'd expect to find leading this charge? Again, not at all. He is soft-spoken, even a bit subdued. Indeed, in his previous position as CEO of International Paper, he was a human-assets leader—a role that may have come more naturally to him. But at Tenneco, the business situation demanded a different approach, and Mead rose to the challenge. That, we argue, is the essence of effective leadership.

Not surprisingly, we also encountered CEOs whose personalities seemed to be a natural fit with their leadership approaches. Herb Kelleher, Southwest Airlines' humorous, down-home CEO, probably could not work in a company that didn't require a human-assets leader. Assertive and demanding, Stephen Friedman, former managing partner of Goldman Sachs, would likely champion change at any organization. How to explain this confluence of personality and leadership approach? We see two possible scenarios. The first is fortunate coincidence: A CEO assesses the business situation, determines which leadership approach is required, and finds that it just happens to reflect his or her personal style. A second and more likely scenario: The CEO is appointed by a person or group of people who make the right match. For instance, a board of directors decides that their organization needs strong strategic direction. What sort of CEO will they look for? Not someone who wants to spend a lot of time guiding and empowering individual employees, but someone who loves to get inside the data, someone with a proved talent for analyzing current market conditions, forecasting future ones, and mapping the route between them.

The board will select a candidate who already acts like a chief strategist. Not surprisingly, given his or her performance in previous positions, the new CEO will continue to use the strategy approach and will be considered a "natural" for the job.

Until scientists discover a gene for leadership—and think of the repercussions of that in business, not to mention politics—the debate about personality will persist. Even if scientists find that leadership is more a case of nurture than of nature, there will still be those who think that only classic General Patton types can lead an organization to success. Our research indicates that leadership is more complicated than that, driven not so much by what someone is like inside but by what the outside demands.

Originally published in May–June 1996
Reprint 96303

The Human Side of
Management

THOMAS TEAL

Executive Summary

SOMETHING ABOUT MANAGEMENT LOOKS SO EASY
that we all think we could succeed where other fail. But
management is really not easy. Managers are expected
to who skill in finance, product development, marketing,
manufacturing, technology, and more. They must be
good at strategy, persuastion, and negotiation. Vision,
fortitude, passion, intelligence, ethical standards,
courage, and tenacity are also de rigueur.

It's no wonder that most managers seem to underperform. Nevertheless, there are a few around who exem-
plify what it takes to achieve greatness. They aren't the
usual suspects we read about. They include the managers many of us know personally.

They are entrepreneurs, heads of divisions, the manager just down the hall. It's time to sing these unsung
heroes. They include the generations of Rosenbluths at

Rosenbluth Travel, who demonstrated the indispensable quality of imagination in reinventing their business again and again. They include Bill Sells of Johns-Manville, who personified integrity in the way he applied to its fiberglass business the harsh lessons of his company's experience with asbestos. They include Ralph Stayer of Johnsonville Sausage, whose determination to overcome his own need for complete control helped make him great. And they include the courageous George Cattabiani of Westinghouse Steam Turbine Division, who threw himself into the lions' den of a hostile labor union and came out with, if not pussycats, at least partners.

Leaders like these are a reminder that greatness involves much more than technique. They are a reminder that it takes managers, not management, to create a great organization.

Look closely at any company in trouble, and you'll probably find that the problem is management. Ask employees about their jobs, and they'll complain about management. Study large corporations, and you'll discover that the biggest barrier to change, innovation, and new ideas is very often management. Make an inventory of the things that have stifled your own creativity and held back your own career; summarize the critical factors that have stood in the way of your organization's success; name the individuals chiefly responsible for the missed opportunities and bungled projects you yourself have witnessed. Managers will top every list.

There is so much inferior management in the world that some people believe we'd be better off in completely flat organizations with no managers at all. Most of us spend the better part of our working lives convinced that we could do the boss's job better than the boss. Something about management looks so easy that we watch one anemic performance after another and never doubt that we could succeed where others repeatedly fail. Of course, a few of us *would* be terrific managers. But just as clearly, most of us would not. We know this is true because so many of us eventually get the chance to try. As for the argument that management is unnecessary, think for a moment about what the world was like before the principles of scientific management rationalized production, democratized wealth, commercialized science, and effectively doubled life expectancy. Good management works miracles.

And still the troublesome fact is that mediocre management is the norm. This is not because some people are born without the management gene or because the wrong people get promoted or because the system can be manipulated—although all these things happen all the time. The overwhelmingly most common explanation is much simpler: capable management is so extraordinarily difficult that few people look good no matter how hard they try. Most of those lackluster managers we all complain about are doing their best to manage well.

In one form or another, managing has become one of the world's most common jobs, and yet we make demands on managers that are nearly impossible to meet. For starters, we ask them to acquire a long list of more or less traditional management skills in finance, cost control, resource allocation, product development, marketing, manufacturing, technology, and a dozen other areas. We also demand that they master the management arts—strategy, persuasion, negotiation, writing, speaking, listening. In addition, we ask them to assume responsibility for organizational success, make a great deal of money, and share it generously. We also require them to demonstrate the qualities that define leadership, integrity, and character—things like vision, fortitude, passion, sensitivity, commitment, insight, intelligence, ethical standards, charisma, luck, courage, tenacity, even from time to time humility. Finally, we insist that they should be our friends, mentors, or guardians, perpetually alert to our best interests. Practicing this common profession adequately, in other words, requires people to display on an everyday basis the combined skills of St. Peter, Peter the Great, and the Great Houdini. No wonder most managers seem to underperform.

And still not all of them do. Easy as it is to point out mediocre managers—and you can hardly swing a cat in the average workplace without hitting several—nearly everyone gets to see a few exemplary managers in the course of a career.

Managing is not a series of mechanical tasks but a set of human interactions.

These people fall into two categories: first, the good or very good managers, who are exceedingly rare because they actually meet the inhuman requirements for adequacy; second, the great managers, or rather the occasional bosses we don't hesitate to call great managers in spite of the fact that they lack a dozen of the skills and virtues that we would normally insist on (and that the job description probably requires). We need to take a closer look at this second category, great managers, because although their numbers are small, they tend to loom exceptionally large in the lives of the people around them.

One reason for the scarcity of managerial greatness is that in educating and training managers, we focus too much on technical proficiency and too little on character. The management sciences—statistics, data analysis, productivity, financial controls, service delivery—are things we can almost take for granted these days. They are subjects we know how to teach. But we're still in the Dark Ages when it comes to teaching people how to behave like great managers—somehow instilling in them capacities such as courage and integrity that can't be taught. Perhaps as a consequence, we've developed a tendency to downplay the importance of the human element in managing. Managers are not responsible for other people's happiness, we say. The workplace isn't a nursery school. We've got market share and growth and profits to worry about, and anyway, power is too useful and entertaining to dribble away on relationships— we've got our own nests to feather. But the only people who become great managers are the ones who understand in their guts that managing is not merely a series of mechanical tasks but a set of human interactions.

In the course of seven years at this magazine, I was lucky enough to come in contact with a surprising number of great managers. As editor of a department we called First Person, I was in a position to help several such people—many of them entrepreneurs or CEOs— tell their own stories about critical problems they had faced, analyzed, grappled with, and sometimes but not always resolved. Not all those stories ended happily, but all of them showed how extraordinarily difficult first-rate management can be. They all showed something else as well—that management is a supremely human activity, a fact that explains why, among all the preposterous demands that we make on managers, character

means more to us than education. We may love and
work hard for a manager who knows too little about
computers or marketing but is a fine human being. We
almost invariably dislike and thwart managers who are
stingy or mean-spirited, however great their technical
abilities. Look back three paragraphs to that long list of
requirements. As it glides upward from acquirable skills
to primal virtues, each item on the list grows less and
less dispensable. Without courage and tenacity, for
example, no manager can *hope* to achieve greatness.
Consider a few of the other absolute prerequisite

Great management requires imagination. If a company's vision and strategy are to differentiate its offer-
ings and create competitive advantage, they must be
original. Original has to mean unconventional, and it
often means counterintuitive. Moreover, it takes ingenuity and wit to bring disparate people and elements
together into a unified but uniquely original whole.
There is even a name for this capacity. It's called
esemplastic imagination, and although it's generally
attributed only to poets, consider the Rosenbluth family.

When Hal Rosenbluth's great-grandfather Marcus
opened a travel business in Philadelphia in 1892, he did
not see himself as just another travel agent. Unlike his
competitors, whose goals were limited to writing and
selling tickets, he saw himself in the immigration
business. For $50, he supplied poor Europeans with
steamship tickets, assistance clearing the hurdles at Ellis
Island, and transport to Philadelphia. And he didn't stop
there. Since immigration was not usually an individual
affair but involved entire families, Marcus Rosenbluth
set himself up as a kind of banker for immigrants as
well. When his immigrants were settled and had jobs, he
collected their savings, five and ten cents at a time, until

there was enough money to bring over a second member of the family and a third and a fourth, until the whole clan was safely in America. From the day it was born, Rosenbluth Travel had the competitive advantage of imagination.

Years later, when immigration slowed (and when the company was forced to give up one of its licenses— travel or banking), Rosenbluth Travel moved into the business of leisure travel. Then in the late 1970s, nearly 90 years after the whole enterprise got off the ground, Hal Rosenbluth took over the business and reinvented it once again. Deregulation had just created turmoil out of order and stability. Between any two given cities, two or three standard airfares had suddenly mushroomed into a chaos of new airlines, schedules, and tariffs, all subject to change without notice. Customers were frustrated and angry trying to figure out what the fares really were, and travel agents, unable to cope or make sense of the confusion, were close to desperation. Hal saw it all as a grand opportunity, partly because he saw that the solution lay in another recent innovation—computers. He sub-scribed to every airline's electronic reservation network (in those days, the airlines charged for access), and he amalgamated all the fares on a computerized system of his own. He bought terminals for his agents and built a new spirit of teamwork using enthusiasm, incentives, and a determination to pay so much attention to his employees' interests that they would feel free to pay attention to the customers'. He guaranteed clients the lowest airfare on every route, and he set out to nail as

Integrity in management means being responsible, communicating clearly, keeping promises, knowing oneself.

many corporate accounts as he could find. But, as Hal put it, "I think our biggest competitive advantage was to understand that as deregulation changed the rules, we were no longer in the travel business as much as we were in the information business." The Rosenbluth imagination was still at work after four generations and nearly 100 years.

Another characteristic of great managers is integrity. All managers believe they behave with integrity, but in practice, many have trouble with the concept. Some think integrity is the same thing as secretiveness or blind loyalty. Others seem to believe it means consistency, even in a bad cause. Some confuse it with discretion and some with the opposite quality—bluntness—or with simply not telling lies. What integrity means in management is more ambitious and difficult than any of these. It means being responsible, of course, but it also means communicating clearly and consistently, being an honest broker, keeping promises, knowing oneself, and avoiding hidden agendas that hang other people out to dry. It comes very close to what we used to call honor, which in part means not telling lies to yourself.

Think of the way Johnson & Johnson dealt with the Tylenol poisoning crisis or how Procter & Gamble withdrew Rely Tampons, a newly launched product, because of an unproved but potentially serious health risk. Compare those cases with the way Johns-Manville handled the asbestos catastrophe. As a Manville manager for more than 30 years, Bill Sells witnessed what he calls "one of the most colossal corporate blunders of the twentieth century." This blunder was not the company's manufacture and sale of asbestos. Companies have been producing deadly chemicals and explosives for hundreds of years. According to Sells, the blunder that killed thousands of people and eliminated an industry was self-deception. Manville managers at every level were simply unwilling to acknowledge the evidence available in the 1940s, when so much of the damage was done, and their capacity for denial held steady through the following decades despite mounting evidence about old and newly identified hazards. The company developed a classic case of bunker mentality: refusing to accept facts; assuming that customers and employees were aware of the hazards and used asbestos at their own risk; denying the need for and the very possibility of change at a company that had successfully hidden its head in the sand for 100 years. Manville funded little medical research, made little effort to communicate what it already knew, and took little or no proactive responsibility for the damage asbestos might do. Captive to the notion that investments that make no product can make no contribution to success, the company pursued only haphazardly the few safety practices that were in place—with tragic consequences for workers' health and decidedly negative effects on maintenance costs, productivity, and profit. Once when he raised objections, Sells was told by his boss, "Bill, you're not loyal," to which he replied, "No, no, you've got it wrong. I'm the one who *is* loyal."

After eight years with the company, Sells was promoted in 1968 to manage a troubled asbestos facility in Illinois, where it was his job to juggle responsibilities that sometimes seemed to conflict—keeping the plant profitable, keeping it productive, and keeping it safe. Slowly and painfully over the next year and a half, he came to understand that labor relations, productivity, dust

Great managers serve two masters: one organizational, one moral.

abatement, profitability, health, and safety were all aspects of the same issue—business integrity—and he launched a half-million-dollar program to replace or rebuild nearly all the safety equipment in the building. By the early 1970s, unfortunately, it was too late to save asbestos or its victims. But Sells did put his insight into practice in the 1980s, when he headed the company's fiberglass division. Among other things, the division funded arm's-length studies and practiced immediate total disclosure (by phone, fax, letter, news conference, videotape, live television, and printed warnings) of everything the company learned about the potential hazards and health risks of the product and made no disingenuous effort to put a procompany spin on the results.

Of course, business integrity means accepting the business consequences of a company's acts, but for great managers, it also means taking personal responsibility. The boss who accused Sells of disloyalty didn't want to hear uncomfortable facts or opposing points of view. But when Sells took over his own division, he opened himself to criticism and argument. This is stressful work for managers, partly because it means serving two masters—one organizational, one moral—and partly because they're not likely to get support for doing it, not even for doing it well. The rewards for great managers are more subtle.

In the early 1980s, William Peace was the general manager of the Synthetic Fuels Division at Westinghouse, a relatively small unit that faced liquidation as a result of declining oil prices unless he could make it attractive enough to sell. In an effort to pare costs, he decided to eliminate a number of the division's 130 jobs because he thought potential buyers would see them as inessential, and, under the circumstances, he had no choice but to lay off the people who held those jobs in spite of their sometimes excellent performance records. He and his department heads drew up the list of 15 positions in a long, emotional meeting, and when it was over and his senior managers were about to go off and convey the bad news, Peace stopped them. He felt this was news he had to communicate himself, in part because he didn't want the entire workforce to conclude that a wave of layoffs was in the making, in part because he felt he owed the individuals involved a face-to-face explanation.

The meeting with the 15 innocent victims the next morning was funereal. People wept openly or stared dejectedly at the floor. Peace walked through his reasoning, insisted that the layoffs were based on job descriptions, not individual performance, and begged the 15 victims to understand if not forgive the need to sacrifice some employees in order to save the division and all its other jobs. They argued, pleaded, and accused him of ingratitude and heartlessness. Peace commiserated, sympathized, accepted their criticism and disapproval, and did his best to give a frank, detailed answer to every question, taking all the heat they cared to give. Gradually the anger faded and the mood shifted from despondency to resignation and even to some grudging understanding and actual interest in the prospects for a sale. Peace recalls it as the most painful meeting he ever took part in. But by the time he shook their hands and wished them luck, he hoped and believed they had come to appreciate his motives if not his choice of sacrificial lambs.

It was months later that he learned how the confrontation had played to those 15 people. A buyer had been found for the division, Peace had been kept on as general manager, and the new owner was investing money in the enterprise. Suddenly Peace was in a position to rehire many of the people he'd laid off, and when he made them the offer, everyone, without exception, came back to work for him, even when it meant giving up good jobs found elsewhere. This is a story about moral and humanitarian compunctions. Equally to the point, however, it's about a manager drawing attention to his own responsibility in adversity, a piece of courage that in this case led to the eventual recapturing of loyal, experienced employees.

Great management has to involve the kind of respect Peace showed for his subordinates, and it must also involve empowerment. The managers people name with admiration are always the ones who delegate their authority, make subordinates feel powerful and capable, and draw from them so much creativity and such a feeling of responsibility that their behavior changes forever. In 1980, when Ricardo Semler took over Semco, his family's business in São Paulo, Brazil—five factories that manufactured, among other things, marine pumps, commercial dishwashers, and mixing equipment for everything from bubble gum to rocket fuel—productivity was low, new contracts were a rarity, and financial disaster loomed. Furthermore, the company was mired in regulations, hierarchy, and distrust. There were intricate rules for travel—strict ceilings on hotel expenses, calls home limited to a set number of minutes, and all the usual red tape about turning in receipts. Factory workers underwent daily theft-prevention security checks, needed permission to use the bathroom, and were generally treated like delinquents.

Semler swept this old world out the door. He reduced the hierarchy to three levels, threw out the rule book (putting in its place what he called the rule of common sense), initiated collegial decision making, and began submitting certain company decisions—such as a factory relocation and several critical acquisitions—to companywide democratic votes. He set up a profit-sharing plan, and, to make it work, he cut the size of the operating units to which it was tied and opened the company's books to everyone on the payroll. On the theory that he should not be sending people he didn't trust around the world to represent his company, he eliminated expense accounting and simply gave people whatever they claimed to have spent. On the theory that it was indecent to treat people like children who in private life were heads of families, civic leaders, and army reserve officers, he put hourly workers on monthly salaries, did away with time clocks and security checks, and let people on the factory floor set their own work goals, methods, and even work hours. He calculated that people whose bonuses depended on profits were neither going to waste the company's money on luxury hotels and cars nor sit around on their hands at work.

He was right. Sales doubled the first year, inventories fell, the company launched eight new products that had been lost in R&D for years, quality improved (for one product, the rejection rate dropped from more than 30% to less than 1%), costs declined, and productivity increased so dramatically that the company was able to reduce the workforce by 32% through attrition and incentives for workers to take early retirement. Semler had reversed the usual practice. Instead of choosing a few responsibilities he could delegate, he picked out a handful of responsibilities that had to remain his own—contracts, strategy, alliances, the authority to make changes in the style of company management—and gave away everything else. Perhaps, he says, some people take advantage of uncontrolled expense accounts or unlocked storage rooms—he would certainly prosecute anyone he found stealing— but his delegation of authority has been so radical and thorough (and effective) that he has no good way of finding out and no desire to know.

In some cases, however, urging people toward shared responsibility and authority is like pulling teeth, and when it means repressing your own instinct to control, like pulling your own teeth. The truth is, people often fail to embrace the opportunities they claim to want, and managers often fail to yield the authority they aim to delegate. Ralph Stayer of Johnsonville Sausage in Wisconsin is another CEO who, in the early 1980s, tried to empower and invigorate his workforce with large helpings of profit sharing and responsibility. But Stayer was his own worst enemy. He was still so deeply in love with his own control that he held onto it in ways that he was not even conscious of. By giving advice to every subordinate who asked him for help in addressing a problem, he continued to run the company and own the problems. By continuing to collect production data, he stayed in charge of production. By continuing to check the quality of the product, he effectively prevented successful delegation of quality control. His subordinates were simply afraid to make decisions unless they knew which decisions he wanted them to make. The only real difference was that now instead of telling them what he wanted, he was making them guess. Not surprisingly, they quickly became experts at correctly interpreting his tone of voice, deciphering his body language, inferring entire policies from a single offhand remark. Once he realized what he was doing and reminded himself that he really *did* want his employees to seize the company reins and own the problems that were wearing him down, he began teaching himself to suppress his own need for control. He fired the one or two direct reports he had trained so well they could hardly act on their own initiative, and he stopped attending the meetings in which production decisions were made or even discussed. Instead, he studied the arts of coaching, teaching, and facilitating, and he altered the job descriptions of managers in order to emphasize those skills even above technical expertise.

The payoff came several years later, when Johnsonville was offered a huge new contract that Stayer didn't believe the company was capable of handling. Rather than simply turn the contract down, however, as he would have done five years earlier, he presented it to his employees. For two weeks, in small groups and at larger team meetings (which Stayer did not attend), they studied the risks and challenges and developed plans to minimize the downside dangers. Ignoring his fears, they accepted and successfully carried out the contract despite the problems it could—and did—add to their lives.

As all these stories illustrate, great management is a continual exercise in learning, education, and persuasion. Getting people to do what's best—for customers, for the business, even for themselves—is often a struggle because it means getting people to *understand* and *want* to do what's best, and that requires integrity, the willingness to empower others, courage, tenacity, and great teaching skills. Sometimes it also requires managers to learn some difficult lessons of their own. Robert Frey, owner of Cin-Made, a small packaging plant in Cincinnati, falls into this category.

Great management requires leaders to learn some difficult lessons of their own.

Frey had no desire to carry all his company's burdens by himself, so, like Ralph Stayer, he decided to share the responsibilities and rewards with his workforce. But his workforce said no thanks. Or rather, not even thanks, just no. They wanted nothing to do with power and self-government even if it really did mean profit sharing on a generous scale, which they very much doubted was the case.

With a partner, Frey had purchased the company in 1984, and at first his relations with employees had been adversarial and hostile. He had openly implied that they were morons, and he had declared their jobs to be easy. Even worse, he had refused them their annual wage hike. They went out on strike but eventually caved in when their war chest ran dry. Frey wouldn't take them back until they'd accepted reduced vacations and a pay cut of 12.5%. Beaten and humiliated, they hated him. He'd won a labor victory, but his prize was a factory full of sullen, angry workers determined to file grievances on every tiny deviation from the contract he had made them sign.

Frey himself soon realized that even if his cost-cutting measures had been necessary, his manner had been arrogant, high-handed, and shortsighted. And he quickly tired of lying awake nights wondering if the company was going to survive. He wanted his employees to take on some of that worrying, and to achieve his end, he was prepared to do whatever it took. In fact, the strike had taught him that his contemptuous treatment of his workers had been a case of extremely poor judgment. The work they did was far from easy, as he'd discovered firsthand when he'd tried to do it himself, and he desperately needed their knowledge of equipment, products, and customers. Whatever his mistakes in the past, he was determined to turn his present predicament on its head and win the confidence and involvement of his workforce. He began consulting their expertise, and he started holding monthly state-of-the-business meetings to let them know exactly where the company stood financially. He also began to study profit-sharing plans. By the end of the contract's first year, the business was again making a profit, and he restored a big piece of the pay cut. Toward the end of its second and final year, he announced that he would restore the remainder and immediately begin a profit-sharing plan that would distribute 30% of pretax profits to employees, half of this to hourly workers. To give the plan teeth, he declared that he would open the company's books to union inspection and audit.

Many, perhaps most, of the hourly workers resisted. They didn't want more responsibility, they didn't want change—he could keep his profits. They wanted higher wages all right, but they wanted guarantees, not risks. Frey was relentless and relentlessly straightforward. He gave new responsibilities to his best people, with merit raises to match, and he found a factory manager who was good at coaxing people to study math and such techniques as statistical process control. He decreed that learning new skills would entitle people to raises. But he firmly refused to increase wages across the board beyond restoring the pay cut that had helped get the company back on its feet. Frey was sure that he and his workforce would continue to be adversaries until they all shared a common interest in the company's success. To that end, he wanted them to understand where wages came from and to grasp the trade-offs between benefits and profits. He wanted them to earn more money than they had ever earned before, but only on the condition that extra money would come from profits:

workers would have to share that portion of the risk and shoulder more responsibility.

He made two public announcements: "I do not choose to own a company that has an adversarial relationship with its employees" and "Employee participation will play an essential role in management." He began losing his temper every time someone refused to participate in decision making or said, "It's not my job." He started using the monthly meetings to share more and more complex information, look at profit projections, and examine numbers such as scrap rates and productivity—areas over which factory workers had direct control. He met with union leaders, told them exactly what he was trying to accomplish, and swore he was not out to break their shop. He ignored resentment, absorbed criticism as his due, delegated relentlessly, even did his best to listen and treat people with visible respect. Some of his workers began to like him. Many began to buy his ideas. Almost all came to believe they could trust what he told them. He explained, taught, learned, pressed nonstop for change, and refused to take no for an answer.

Gradually over the course of several years, the struggle began to pay off. Profits grew (individual profit shares over a four-year period averaged out to a 36% increment to wages), productivity rose 30%, absenteeism fell to nearly zero, and grievances declined to one or two per year. More important for Frey, workers began to make the connection between income and initiative, and today they carry out all the long-term planning and management of labor, materials, equipment, production runs, packing, and delivery. Perhaps best of all from Frey's point of view, some of them probably lie awake nights worrying about company performance.

Frey is an interesting case of a great manager who has great flaws that somehow just don't matter. Tact is not on the list of indispensable ingredients; neither is elegance. But there is one more indispensable capacity, and Frey possesses it, although in an unusually unpolished form: the capacity to create excitement. We generally call it the ability to motivate people, but that phrase is too bloodless to suggest the adrenaline that's needed to build great companies. Frey stirred people up, first to anger, it's true, but later to enterprise and creativity as well.

We want all our leaders—from politicians to movie stars—to stir our souls a little, and we want the same thing from our managers. They have become the most significant figures in our society, with as central a role to play as generals, lords, oracles, or politicians played in centuries past, and we look to them for more than guidance.

Great management involves courage and tenacity. It closely resembles heroism.

These few stories can't possibly paint a comprehensive picture of great management in action, but they do give us a rough sketch of the objective, which is to magnify the social core of human nature, bring individual talents to fruition, create value, and combine those activities with enough passion to generate the greatest possible advantages for every player.

Which brings me to another observation about great managers, this one a little more extravagant. We've already noted that most of us demand something in a manager that is larger than life, and I suggest that in really great managers, we get it. Great managers are distinguished by something more than insight, integrity, leadership, and imagination, and that something more (part of it is tenacity; much of the rest is plain courage) bears a close resemblance to heroism.

Now, people whose concept of the heroic is inextricably tied to burning buildings and reckless self-sacrifice may find this suggestion offensive. Heroism certainly isn't a word we're comfortable using in the same breath with the word self-interest, and there's no escaping the fact that managers do what they do at least partially to serve themselves, even to make money, even to make a lot of money. Still and all, creating value where none existed; saving and creating jobs and careers and lifetime goals; doing what's right, productive, and beneficial; standing alone, often without support, often against formidable opposition; doing the hard intellectual work of conceiving a vision and the hard moral work of staying true to it—aren't these the kinds of acts we associate with heroism? Even if there *are* rewards? Even if the eventual rewards are great? For that matter, don't quite a few of our traditional storybook heroes—and our modern media heroes as well—reap lavish benefits? Half the kingdom, wealth, fame, a seat in the Senate, the presidency?

One of the most striking things about entrepreneurs, for example, is their sometimes awkward resemblance to Romantic heroes—their isolation, the fact that they are perpetually swimming against the current, against the wishes of one or more of their constituencies, against convention, against criticism, against heavy odds. Management at its finest has a heroic dimension because it deals with eternal human challenges and offers no excuse for failure and no escape from responsibility. Managers can be as thoughtless and selfish as any other human beings, but they can also be as idealistic and as noble.

Great managers also bring forth other great managers. William Peace, who confronted the employees he was about to lay off, tells a second story—one about a general manager named Gene Cattabiani, who had been his boss years earlier and who shaped the kind of manager Peace himself became. In the early 1970s, when the story took place, Cattabiani had just taken over the Westinghouse Steam Turbine Division in Philadelphia and faced serious problems. The division was not making money, and to save it, he needed to reduce costs and raise productivity. Yet the greatest room for improvement was on the factory floor, and the animosities between management and labor were intense. Union leaders had a reputation for intransigence, and several strikes had grown violent. On the other side, management saw labor as lazy and selfish, and it tended to treat workers with contempt. Cattabiani felt the time had come to break the impasse. Union cooperation was the key to the kind of change that could save the division, and he was determined to change attitudes and begin treating the workforce with respect and honesty. The method he chose was an unprecedented series of presentations to the entire labor force on the state of the business, with slides and a question-and-answer period. Against the better judgment of his immediate subordinates, he decided to make the presentations himself, and because the workforce numbered in the hundreds, he would have to repeat the talk several times.

The first presentation was a trial by fire. He wanted employees to see that the division was in trouble and that their very jobs depended on a new kind of management-labor relationship. But they saw Cattabiani as the enemy. They subjected him to catcalls, heckling, and open abuse, and it was not at all clear that they heard a

word of his careful explanations. Peace and his colleagues were convinced he would see that the presentations were a mistake and cancel the rest of the series or
ask someone else to do them. But with obvious dread, he
persisted. Again and again, he exposed himself to the
insults and epithets of people who didn't seem to believe
a word he said. Afterward, he began to make regular vis-
its to the shop floor, a thing none of his predecessors
had ever done, and to banter and reason with the worst
of his hecklers. As the weeks went by, the workers he
spoke to began to nod to him when he appeared, to listen to what he had to say, and then to argue with him
face to face. Gradually, in the midst of open animosity,
the change that Cattabiani wanted began to take place.
He ceased to be an ordinary useless manager and
became a creature of flesh and blood. He acquired credibility, and a dialogue developed where before there had
been nothing but grim silence or hostility.

The presentations and their aftermath were a water-
shed. Painful and lonely as the process was for Cattabiani, it gave him a human status that no manager had
previously held. The workers wanted to confront the
source of their problems. By giving them that opportunity, Cattabiani made himself difficult to demonize and
impossible to dismiss, and from that moment forward,
labor-management relations took a sharp turn for the
better. Over the following months, he made big changes
in the way the division was run. He introduced greater
work flexibility, instituted higher standards for quality
and productivity, and when necessary, laid people off.
Each improvement was a new struggle, but Cattabiani
continued to make himself a disarmingly open target for
anger and argument, the necessary changes did take
place, peace was maintained, and the division's per-

formance improved more than enough to save its life and the hundreds of jobs it provided.

It is hard to read stories like this one and the one about Cattabiani's protégé, William Peace, and not get a sense that these two men and a great many men and women like them, at least brush the edges of something genuinely gallant, however industrial, however small the scale. Management is terrifically difficult. It takes exceptional, sometimes heroic people to do it well. But even doing it well *enough* is a much more honorable and arduous task than we commonly suppose.

Originally published in November–December 1996
Reprint 96610

This article is adapted from the introduction to Thomas Teal's book First Person: Tales of Management Courage and Tenacity *(Harvard Business School Press, 1996).*

The Work of Leadership

RONALD A. HEIFETZ AND

DONALD L. LAURIE

Executive Summary

MORE AND MORE COMPANIES TODAY are facing adaptive challenges: changes in societies, markets, and technology around the globe are forcing them to clarify their values, develop new strategies, and learn new ways of operating. And the most important task for leaders in the face of such challenges is mobilizing people throughout the organization to do adaptive work.

Yet for many senior executives, providing such leadership is difficult. Why? One reason is that they are accustomed to solving problems themselves. Another is that adaptive change is distressing for the people going through it. They need to take on new roles, relationships, values, and approaches to work. Many employees are ambivalent about the sacrifices required of them and look to senior executives to take problems off their shoulders.

But both sets of expectations have to be unlearned. Rather than providing answers, leaders have to ask tough questions. Rather than protecting people from outside threats, leaders should let the pinch of reality stimulate them to adapt. Instead of orienting people to their current roles, leaders must disorient them so that new relationships can develop. Instead of quelling conflict, leaders should draw the issues out. Instead of maintaining norms, leaders must challenge "the way we do business" and help others distinguish immutable values from the historical practices that have become obsolete.

The authors offer six principles for leading adaptive work: "getting on the balcony," identifying the adaptive challenge, regulating distress, maintaining disciplined attention, giving the work back to people, and protecting voices of leadership from below.

To stay alive, Jack Pritchard had to change his life. Triple bypass surgery and medication could help, the heart surgeon told him, but no technical fix could release Pritchard from his own responsibility for changing the habits of a lifetime. He had to stop smoking, improve his diet, get some exercise, and take time to relax, remembering to breathe more deeply each day. Pritchard's doctor could provide sustaining technical expertise and take supportive action, but only Pritchard could adapt his ingrained habits to improve his long-term health. The doctor faced the leadership task of mobilizing the patient to make critical behavioral changes; Jack Pritchard faced the adaptive work of figuring out which specific changes to make and how to incorporate them into his daily life.

Companies today face challenges similar to the ones confronting Pritchard and his doctor. They face *adaptive challenges.* Changes in societies, markets, customers, competition, and technology around the globe are forcing organizations to clarify their values, develop new strategies, and learn new ways of operating. Often the toughest task for leaders in effecting change is mobilizing people throughout the organization to do adaptive work.

Adaptive work is required when our deeply held beliefs are challenged, when the values that made us successful become less relevant, and when legitimate yet competing perspectives emerge. We see adaptive challenges every day at every level of the workplace—when companies restructure or reengineer, develop or implement strategy, or merge businesses. We see adaptive

Solutions to adaptive challenges reside not in the executive suite but in the collective intelligence of employees at all levels.

challenges when marketing has difficulty working with operations, when cross-functional teams don't work well, or when senior executives complain, "We don't seem to be able to execute effectively." Adaptive problems are often systemic problems with no ready answers.

Mobilizing an organization to adapt its behaviors in order to thrive in new business environments is critical. Without such change, any company today would falter. Indeed, getting people to do adaptive work is the mark of leadership in a competitive world. Yet for most senior executives, providing leadership and not just authoritative expertise is extremely difficult. Why? We see two reasons. First, in order to make change happen, executives have to break a long-standing behavior pattern of their own: providing leadership in the form of solutions. This tendency is quite natural because many executives reach their positions of authority by virtue of their competence in taking responsibility and solving problems. But the locus of responsibility for problem solving when a company faces an adaptive challenge must shift to its people. Solutions to adaptive challenges reside not in the executive suite but in the collective intelligence of employees at all levels, who need to use one another as resources, often across boundaries, and learn their way to those solutions.

Second, adaptive change is distressing for the people going through it. They need to take on new roles, new relationships, new values, new behaviors, and new approaches to work. Many employees are ambivalent about the efforts and sacrifices required of them. They often look to the senior executive to take problems off their shoulders. But those expectations have to be unlearned. Rather than fulfilling the expectation that they will provide answers, leaders have to ask tough questions. Rather than protecting people from outside threats, leaders should allow them to feel the pinch of reality in order to stimulate them to adapt. Instead of orienting people to their current roles, leaders must disorient them so that new relationships can develop. Instead of quelling conflict, leaders have to draw the issues out. Instead of maintaining norms, leaders have to challenge "the way we do business" and help others distinguish immutable values from historical practices that must go.

Drawing on our experience with managers from around the world, we offer six principles for leading adaptive work: "getting on the balcony," identifying the adaptive challenge, regulating distress, maintaining disciplined attention, giving the work back to people, and protecting voices of leadership from below. We illustrate those principles with an example of adaptive change at KPMG Netherlands, a professional-services firm.

Get on the Balcony

Earvin "Magic" Johnson's greatness in leading his basketball team came in part from his ability to play hard while keeping the whole game situation in mind, as if he stood in a press box or on a balcony above the field of play. Bobby Orr played hockey in the same way. Other players might fail to recognize the larger patterns of play that performers like Johnson and Orr quickly understand, because they are so engaged in the game that they get carried away by it. Their attention is captured by the rapid motion, the physical contact, the roar of the crowd, and the pressure to execute. In sports, most players simply may not see who is open for a pass, who is missing a block, or how the offense and defense work together. Players like Johnson and Orr watch these things and allow their observations to guide their actions.

Business leaders have to be able to view patterns as if they were on a balcony. It does them no good to be swept up in the field of action. Leaders have to see a context for change or create one. They should give employees a strong sense of the history of the enterprise and what's good about its past, as well as an idea of the market forces at work today and the responsibility people must take in shaping the future. Leaders must be able to identify struggles over values and power, recognize patterns of work avoidance, and watch for the many other functional and dysfunctional reactions to change.

Without the capacity to move back and forth between the field of action and the balcony, to reflect day to day, moment to moment, on the many ways in which an organization's habits can sabotage adaptive work, a leader easily and unwittingly becomes a prisoner of the system. The dynamics of adaptive change are far too complex to keep track of, let alone influence, if leaders stay only on the field of play.

We have encountered several leaders, some of whom we discuss in this article, who manage to spend much of their precious time on the balcony as they guide their organizations through change. Without that perspective, they probably would have been unable to mobilize people to do adaptive work. Getting on the balcony is thus a prerequisite for following the next five principles.

Identify the Adaptive Challenge

When a leopard threatens a band of chimpanzees, the leopard rarely succeeds in picking off a stray. Chimps know how to respond to this kind of threat. But when a man with an automatic rifle comes near, the routine responses fail. Chimps risk extinction in a world of poachers unless they figure out how to disarm the new threat. Similarly, when businesses cannot learn quickly to adapt to new challenges, they are likely to face their own form of extinction.

Consider the well-known case of British Airways. Having observed the revolutionary changes in the airline industry during the 1980s, then chief executive Colin Marshall clearly recognized the need to transform an airline nicknamed Bloody Awful by its own passengers into an exemplar of customer service. He also understood that this ambition would require more than anything else changes in values, practices, and relationships throughout the company. An organization whose people clung to functional silos and valued pleasing their bosses more than pleasing customers could not become The World's Favourite Airline. Marshall needed an organization dedicated to serving people, acting on trust, respecting the individual, and making teamwork happen across boundaries. Values had to change throughout British Airways. People had to learn to collaborate and to develop a collective sense of responsibility for the direction and performance of the airline. Marshall identified the essential adaptive challenge: creating trust throughout the organization. He is one of the first executives we have known to make "creating trust" a priority.

To lead British Airways, Marshall had to get his executive team to understand the nature of the threat created by dissatisfied customers: Did it represent a technical challenge or an adaptive challenge? Would expert advice and technical adjustments within basic routines suffice, or would people throughout the company have to learn new ways of doing business, develop new competencies, and begin to work collectively?

Marshall and his team set out to diagnose in more detail the organization's challenges. They looked in three places. First, they listened to the ideas and concerns of people inside and outside the organization—meeting with crews on flights, showing up in the 350-person reservation center in New York, wandering around the baggage-handling area in Tokyo, or visiting the passenger lounge in whatever airport they happened to be in. Their primary questions were, Whose values, beliefs, attitudes, or behaviors would have to change in order for progress to take place? What shifts in priorities, resources, and power were necessary? What sacrifices would have to be made and by whom?

Second, Marshall and his team saw conflicts as clues—symptoms of adaptive challenges. The way conflicts across functions were being expressed were mere surface phenomena: the underlying conflicts had to be diagnosed. Disputes over seemingly technical issues such as procedures, schedules, and lines of authority were in fact proxies for underlying conflicts about values and norms.

Third, Marshall and his team held a mirror up to themselves, recognizing that they embodied the adaptive challenges facing the organization. Early in the transformation of British Airways, competing values and norms were played out on the executive team in dysfunctional ways that impaired the capacity of the rest of the company to collaborate across functions and units and make the necessary trade-offs. No executive can hide from the fact that his or her team reflects the best and the worst of the company's values and norms, and therefore provides a case in point for insight into the nature of the adaptive work ahead.

Thus, identifying its adaptive challenge was crucial in British Airways' bid to become The World's Favourite Airline. For the strategy to succeed, the company's leaders needed to understand themselves, their people, and the potential sources of conflict. Marshall recognized that strategy development itself requires adaptive work.

Regulate Distress

Adaptive work generates distress. Before putting people to work on challenges for which there are no ready solutions, a leader must realize that people can learn only so much so fast. At the same time, they must feel the need to change as reality brings new challenges. They cannot learn new ways when they are overwhelmed, but eliminating stress altogether removes the impetus for doing adaptive work. Because a leader must strike a delicate balance between having people feel the need to change and having them feel overwhelmed by change, leadership is a razor's edge.

A leader must attend to three fundamental tasks in order to help maintain a productive level of tension. Adhering to these tasks will allow him or her to motivate people without disabling them.

First, a leader must create what can be called a holding environment. To use the analogy of a pressure cooker, a leader needs to regulate the pressure by turning up the heat while also allowing some steam to escape. If the pressure exceeds the cooker's capacity, the cooker can blow up. However, nothing cooks without some heat.

In the early stages of corporate change, the holding environment can be a temporary "place" in which a leader creates the conditions for diverse groups to talk to one another about the challenges facing them, to frame and debate issues, and to clarify the assumptions behind competing perspectives and values. Over time, more issues can be phased in as they become ripe. At British Airways, for example, the shift from an internal focus to a customer focus took place over four or five years and dealt with important issues in succession: building a credible executive team, communicating with a highly fragmented organization, defining new measures of performance and compensation, and developing sophisticated information systems. During that time, employees at all levels learned to identify what and how they needed to change.

Thus a leader must sequence and pace the work. Too often, senior managers convey that everything is important. They start new initiatives without stopping other activities or they start too many initiatives at the same time. They overwhelm and disorient the very people who need to take responsibility for the work.

Second, a leader is responsible for direction, protection, orientation, managing conflict, and shaping norms. (See the table "Adaptive Work Calls for Leadership.") Fulfilling these responsibilities is also important for a manager in technical or routine situations. But a leader engaged in adaptive work uses his authority to fulfill them differently. A leader provides direction by identifying the organization's adaptive challenge and framing the key questions and issues. A leader protects people by

Adaptive Work Calls for Leadership

Responsibilities	Situation	
	Technical or Routine	Adaptive
Direction	Define problems and provide solutions	Identify the adaptive challenge and frame key questions and issues
Protection	Shield the organization from external threats	Let the organization feel external pressures within a range it can stand
Orientation	Clarify roles and responsibilities	Challenge current roles and resist pressure to define new roles quickly
Managing Conflict	Restore order	Expose conflict or let it emerge
Shaping Norms	Maintain norms	Challenge unproductive norms

managing the rate of change. A leader orients people to new roles and responsibilities by clarifying business realities and key values. A leader helps expose conflict, viewing it as the engine of creativity and learning. Finally, a leader helps the organization maintain those norms that must endure and challenge those that need to change.

Third, a leader must have presence and poise; regulating distress is perhaps a leader's most difficult job. The pressures to restore equilibrium are enormous. Just as molecules bang hard against the walls of a pressure cooker, people bang up against leaders who are trying to sustain the pressures of tough, conflict-filled work. Although leadership demands a deep understanding of the pain of change—the fears and sacrifices associated with major readjustment—it also requires the ability to hold steady and maintain the tension. Otherwise, the pressure escapes and the stimulus for learning and change is lost.

A leader has to have the emotional capacity to tolerate uncertainty, frustration, and pain. He has to be able to raise tough questions without getting too anxious himself. Employees as well as colleagues and customers will carefully observe verbal and nonverbal cues to a leader's ability to hold steady. He needs to communicate confidence that he and they can tackle the tasks ahead.

Maintain Disciplined Attention

Different people within the same organization bring different experiences, assumptions, values, beliefs, and habits to their work. This diversity is valuable because innovation and learning are the products of differences. No one learns anything without being open to contrasting points of view. Yet managers at all levels are often unwilling—or unable—to address their competing perspectives collectively. They frequently avoid paying attention to issues that disturb them. They restore equilibrium quickly, often with work avoidance maneuvers. A leader must get employees to confront tough trade-offs in values, procedures, operating styles, and power.

That is as true at the top of the organization as it is in the middle or on the front line. Indeed, if the executive team cannot model adaptive work, the organization will languish. If senior managers can't draw out and deal with divisive issues, how will people elsewhere in the organization change their behaviors and rework their relationships? As Jan Carlzon, the legendary CEO of Scandinavian Airlines System (SAS), told us, "One of the most interesting missions of leadership is getting people on the executive team to listen to and learn from one another. Held in debate, people can learn their way to collective solutions when they understand one another's assumptions. The work of the leader is to get conflict out into the open and use it as a source of creativity."

Because work avoidance is rampant in organizations, a leader has to counteract distractions that prevent people from dealing with adaptive issues. Scapegoating, denial, focusing only on today's technical issues, or attacking individuals rather than the perspectives they represent—all forms of work avoidance—are to be expected when an organization undertakes adaptive work. Distractions have to be identified when they occur so that people will regain focus.

When sterile conflict takes the place of dialogue, a leader has to step in and put the team to work on reframing the issues. She has to deepen the debate with questions, unbundling the issues into their parts rather than letting conflict remain polarized and superficial.

When people preoccupy themselves with blaming external forces, higher management, or a heavy workload, a leader has to sharpen the team's sense of responsibility for carving out the time to press forward. When the team fragments and individuals resort to protecting their own turf, leaders have to demonstrate the need for collaboration. People have to discover the value of consulting with one another and using one another as resources in the problem-solving process. For example, one CEO we know uses executive meetings, even those that focus on operational and technical issues, as opportunities to teach the team how to work collectively on adaptive problems.

Of course, only the rare manager *intends* to avoid adaptive work. In general, people feel ambivalent about it. Although they want to make progress on hard problems or live up to their renewed and clarified values, people also want to avoid the associated distress. Just as millions of U.S. citizens want to reduce the federal budget deficit, but not by giving up their tax dollars or benefits or jobs, so, too, managers may consider adaptive work a priority but have difficulty sacrificing their familiar ways of doing business.

People need leadership to help them maintain their focus on the tough questions. Disciplined attention is the currency of leadership.

Give the Work Back to People

Everyone in the organization has special access to information that comes from his or her particular vantage point. Everyone may see different needs and opportunities. People who sense early changes in the marketplace are often at the periphery, but the organization will thrive if it can bring that information to bear on tactical and strategic decisions. When people do not act on their special knowledge, businesses fail to adapt.

All too often, people look up the chain of command, expecting senior management to meet market challenges for which they themselves are responsible. Indeed, the greater and more persistent distresses that accompany adaptive work make such dependence worse. People tend to become passive, and senior managers who pride themselves on being problem solvers take decisive action. That behavior restores equilibrium in the short term but ultimately leads to complacency and habits of work avoidance that shield people from responsibility, pain, and the need to change.

Getting people to assume greater responsibility is not easy. Not only are many lower-level employees comfortable being told what to do, but many managers are accustomed to treating subordinates like machinery requiring control. Letting people take the initiative in defining and solving problems means that management needs to learn to support rather than control. Workers, for their part, need to learn to take responsibility.

Jan Carlzon encouraged responsibility taking at SAS by trusting others and decentralizing authority. A leader has to let people bear the weight of responsibility. "The key is to let them discover the problem," he said. "You won't be successful if people aren't carrying the recognition of the problem and the solution within themselves." To that end, Carlzon sought widespread engagement.

For example, in his first two years at SAS, Carlzon spent up to 50% of his time communicating directly in large meetings and indirectly in a host of innovative ways: through workshops, brainstorming sessions, learning exercises, newsletters, brochures, and exposure in the public media. He demonstrated through a variety of symbolic acts—for example, by eliminating the pretentious executive dining room and burning thousands of pages of manuals and handbooks—the extent to which rules had come to dominate the company. He made himself a pervasive presence, meeting with and listening to people both inside and outside the organization. He even wrote a book, *Moments of Truth* (Ballinger, 1987), to explain his values, philosophy, and strategy. As Carlzon noted, "If no one else read it, at least my people would."

A leader also must develop collective self-confidence. Again, Carlzon said it well: "People aren't born with self-confidence. Even the most self-confident people can be broken. Self-confidence comes from success, experience, and the organization's environment. The leader's most important role is to instill confidence in people. They must dare to take risks and responsibility. You must back them up if they make mistakes."

Protect Voices of Leadership from Below

Giving a voice to all people is the foundation of an organization that is willing to experiment and learn. But, in fact, whistle-blowers, creative deviants, and other such original voices routinely get smashed and silenced in organizational life. They generate disequilibrium, and the easiest way for an organization to restore equilibrium is to neutralize those voices, sometimes in the name of teamwork and "alignment."

The voices from below are usually not as articulate as one would wish. People speaking beyond their authority usually feel self-conscious and sometimes have to generate "too much" passion to get themselves geared up for speaking out. Of course, that often makes it harder for them to communicate effectively. They pick the wrong time and place, and often bypass proper channels of communication and lines of authority. But buried inside a poorly packaged interjection may lie an important intuition that needs to be teased out and considered. To toss it out for its bad timing, lack of clarity, or seeming unreasonableness is to lose potentially valuable information and discourage a potential leader in the organization.

That is what happened to David, a manager in a large manufacturing company. He had listened when his superiors encouraged people to look for problems, speak openly, and take responsibility. So he raised an issue about one of the CEO's pet projects—an issue that was "too hot to handle" and had been swept under the carpet for years. Everyone understood that it was not open to discussion, but David knew that proceeding with the project could damage or derail key elements of the company's overall strategy. He raised the issue directly in a meeting with his boss and the CEO. He provided a clear description of the problem, a rundown of competing perspectives, and a summary of the consequences of continuing to pursue the project.

The CEO angrily squelched the discussion and reinforced the positive aspects of his pet project. When David and his boss left the room, his boss exploded: "Who do you think you are, with your holier-than-thou attitude?" He insinuated that David had never liked the CEO's pet project because David hadn't come up with the idea himself. The subject was closed.

David had greater expertise in the area of the project than either his boss or the CEO. But his two superiors showed no curiosity, no effort to investigate David's reasoning, no awareness that he was behaving responsibly with the interests of the company at heart. It rapidly became clear to David that it was more important to understand what mattered to the boss than to focus on real issues. The CEO and David's boss together squashed the viewpoint of a leader from below and thereby killed his potential for leadership in the organization. He would either leave the company or never go against the grain again.

Leaders must rely on others within the business to raise questions that may indicate an impending adaptive challenge. They have to provide cover to people who point to the internal contradictions of the enterprise.

Leaders have to provide cover to employees who point to the internal contradictions of the enterprise.

Those individuals often have the perspective to provoke rethinking that people in authority do not. Thus, as a rule of thumb, when authority figures feel the reflexive urge to glare at or otherwise silence someone, they should resist. The urge to restore social equilibrium is quite powerful, and it comes on fast. One has to get accustomed to getting on the balcony, delaying the impulse, and asking, What *really* is this guy talking about? Is there something we're missing?

Doing Adaptive Work at KPMG Netherlands

The highly successful KPMG Netherlands provides a good example of how a company can engage in adaptive work. In 1994, Ruud Koedijk, the firm's chairman, recognized a strategic challenge. Although the auditing, consulting, and tax-preparation partnership was the industry leader in the Netherlands and was highly profitable, growth opportunities in the segments it served were limited. Margins in the auditing business were being squeezed as the market became more saturated, and competition in the consulting business was increasing as well. Koedijk knew that the firm needed to move into more profitable growth areas, but he didn't know what they were or how KPMG might identify them.

Koedijk and his board were confident that they had the tools to do the analytical strategy work: analyze trends and discontinuities, understand core competencies, assess their competitive position, and map potential opportunities. They were considerably less certain that they could commit to implementing the strategy that would emerge from their work. Historically, the partnership had resisted attempts to change, basically because the partners were content with the way things were. They had been successful for a long time, so they saw no reason to learn new ways of doing business, either from their fellow partners or from anyone lower down in the organization. Overturning the partners' attitude and its deep impact on the organization's culture posed an enormous adaptive challenge for KPMG.

Koedijk could see from the balcony that the very structure of KPMG inhibited change. In truth, KPMG was less a partnership than a collection of small fiefdoms in which each partner was a lord. The firm's success was the cumulative accomplishment of each of the individual partners, not the unified result of 300 colleagues pulling together toward a shared ambition. Success was measured solely in terms of the profitability of individual units. As one partner described it, "If the bottom line was correct, you were a 'good fellow.'" As a result, one partner would not trespass on another's turf, and learning from others was a rare event. Because independence was so highly valued, confrontations were rare and conflict was camouflaged. If partners wanted to resist firmwide change, they did not kill the issue directly. "Say yes, do no" was the operative phrase.

Koedijk also knew that this sense of autonomy got in the way of developing new talent at KPMG. Directors rewarded their subordinates for two things: not making mistakes and delivering a high number of billable hours per week. The emphasis was not on creativity or innovation. Partners were looking for errors when they reviewed their subordinates' work, not for new understanding or fresh insight. Although Koedijk could see the broad outlines of the adaptive challenges facing his organization, he knew that he could not mandate behavioral change. What he could do was create the conditions for people to discover for themselves how they needed to change. He set a process in motion to make that happen.

To start, Koedijk held a meeting of all 300 partners and focused their attention on the history of KPMG, the current business reality, and the business issues they could expect to face. He then raised the question of how they would go about changing as a firm and asked for their perspectives on the issues. By launching the strategic initiative through dialogue rather than edict, he built trust within the partner ranks. Based on this emerging trust and his own credibility, Koedijk persuaded the partners to release 100 partners and nonpartners from their day-to-day responsibilities to work on the strategic challenges. They would devote 60% of their time for nearly four months to that work.

Koedijk and his colleagues established a strategic integration team of 12 senior partners to work with the 100 professionals (called "the 100") from different levels and disciplines. Engaging people below the rank of partner in a major strategic initiative was unheard of and signaled a new approach from the start: many of these people's opinions had never before been valued or sought by authority figures in the firm. Divided into 14 task forces, the 100 were to work in three areas: gauging future trends and discontinuities, defining core competencies, and grappling with the adaptive challenges facing the organization. They were housed on a separate floor with their own support staff, and they were unfettered by traditional rules and regulations. Hennie Both, KPMG's director of marketing and communications, signed on as project manager.

As the strategy work got under way, the task forces had to confront the existing KPMG culture. Why? Because they literally could not do their new work within the old rules. They could not work when strong respect for the individual came at the expense of effective teamwork, when deeply held individual beliefs got in the way of genuine discussion, and when unit loyalties formed a barrier to cross-functional problem solving. Worst of all, task force members found themselves avoiding conflict and unable to discuss those problems. A number of the task forces became dysfunctional and unable to do their strategy work.

To focus their attention on what needed to change, Both helped the task forces map the culture they desired against the current culture. They discovered very little overlap. The top descriptors of the current culture were: develop opposing views, demand perfection, and avoid conflict. The top characteristics of the desired culture were: create the opportunity for self-fulfillment, develop a caring environment, and maintain trusting relations with colleagues. Articulating this gap made tangible for the group the adaptive challenge that Koedijk saw facing KPMG. In other words, *the people who needed to do the changing had finally framed the adaptive challenge for themselves*: How could KPMG succeed at a competence-based strategy that depended on cooperation across multiple units and layers if its people couldn't succeed in these task forces? Armed with that understanding, the task force members could become emissaries to the rest of the firm.

On a more personal level, each member was asked to identify his or her *individual* adaptive challenge. What attitudes, behaviors, or habits did each one need to change, and what specific actions would he or she take? Who else needed to be involved for individual change to take root? Acting as coaches and consultants, the task force members gave one another supportive feedback and suggestions. They had learned to confide, to listen, and to advise with genuine care.

Progress on these issues raised the level of trust dramatically, and task force members began to understand what adapting their behavior meant in everyday terms. They understood how to identify an adaptive issue and developed a language with which to discuss what they needed to do to improve their collective ability to solve problems. They talked about dialogue, work avoidance, and using the collective intelligence of the group. They knew how to "call" one another on dysfunctional behavior. They had begun to develop the culture required to implement the new business strategy.

Despite the critical breakthroughs toward developing a collective understanding of the adaptive challenge, regulating the level of distress was a constant preoccupation for Koedijk, the board, and Both. The nature of the work was distressing. Strategy work means broad assignments with limited instructions; at KPMG, people were accustomed to highly structured assignments. Strategy work also means being creative. At one breakfast meeting, a board member stood on a table to challenge the group to be more creative and toss aside old

The task forces compared the old KPMG to a sluggish hippo and the new one to a dolphin—playful and eager to learn.

rules. This radical and unexpected behavior further raised the distress level: no one had ever seen a partner behave this way before. People realized that their work experience had prepared them only for performing routine tasks with people "like them" from their own units.

The process allowed for conflict and focused people's attention on the hot issues in order to help them learn how to work with conflict in a constructive manner. But the heat was kept within a tolerable range in some of the following ways:

- On one occasion when tensions were unusually high, the 100 were brought together to voice their concerns to the board in an Oprah Winfrey-style meeting. The board sat in the center of an auditorium and took pointed questions from the surrounding group.

- The group devised sanctions to discourage unwanted behavior. In the soccer-crazy Netherlands, all participants in the process were issued the yellow cards that soccer referees use to indicate "foul" to offending players. They used the cards to stop the action when someone started arguing his or her point without listening to or understanding the assumptions and competing perspectives of other participants.

- The group created symbols. They compared the old KPMG to a hippopotamus that was large and cumbersome, liked to sleep a lot, and became aggressive when its normal habits were disturbed. They aspired to be dolphins, which they characterized as playful, eager to learn, and happily willing to go the extra mile for the team. They even paid attention to the statement that clothes make: it surprised some clients to see managers wandering through the KPMG offices that summer in Bermuda shorts and T-shirts.

- The group made a deliberate point of having fun. "Playtime" could mean long bicycle rides or laser-gun games at a local amusement center. In one spontaneous moment at the KPMG offices, a discussion of the power of people mobilized toward a common goal led the group to go outside and use their collective leverage to move a seemingly immovable concrete block.

- The group attended frequent two- and three-day off-site meetings to help bring closure to parts of the work.

These actions, taken as a whole, changed attitudes and behaviors. Curiosity became more valued than obedience to rules. People no longer deferred to the senior authority figure in the room; genuine dialogue neutralized hierarchical power in the battle over ideas. The tendency for each individual to promote his or her pet solution gave way to understanding other perspectives. A confidence in the ability of people in different units to work together and work things out emerged. The people with the most curious minds and interesting questions soon became the most respected.

As a result of confronting strategic and adaptive challenges, KPMG as a whole will move from auditing to assurance, from operations consulting to shaping corporate vision, from business-process reengineering to developing organizational capabilities, and from teaching traditional skills to its own clients to creating learning organizations. The task forces identified $50 million to $60 million worth of new business opportunities.

Many senior partners who had believed that a firm dominated by the auditing mentality could not contain creative people were surprised when the process unlocked creativity, passion, imagination, and a willingness to take risks. Two stories illustrate the fundamental changes that took place in the firm's mind-set.

We saw one middle manager develop the confidence to create a new business. He spotted the opportunity to provide KPMG services to virtual organizations and strategic alliances. He traveled the world, visiting the leaders of 65 virtual organizations. The results of his innovative research served as a resource to KPMG in

Many managers treat adaptive challenges as if they were technical problems.

entering this growing market. Moreover, he represented the new KPMG by giving a keynote address discussing his findings at a world forum. We also saw a 28-year-old female auditor skillfully guide a group of older, male senior partners through a complex day of looking at opportunities associated with implementing the firm's new strategies. That could not have occurred the year before. The senior partners never would have listened to such a voice from below.

Leadership as Learning

Many efforts to transform organizations through mergers and acquisitions, restructuring, reengineering, and strategy work falter because managers fail to grasp the requirements of adaptive work. They make the classic error of treating adaptive challenges like technical problems that can be solved by tough-minded senior executives.

The implications of that error go to the heart of the work of leaders in organizations today. Leaders crafting strategy have access to the technical expertise and the tools they need to calculate the benefits of a merger or restructuring, understand future trends and discontinuities, identify opportunities, map existing competencies, and identify the steering mechanisms to support their strategic direction. These tools and techniques are readily available both within organizations and from a variety of consulting firms, and they are very useful. In many cases, however, seemingly good strategies fail to be implemented. And often the failure is misdiagnosed: "We had a good strategy, but we couldn't execute it effectively."

In fact, the strategy itself is often deficient because too many perspectives were ignored during its formulation. The failure to do the necessary adaptive work during the strategy development process is a symptom of senior managers' technical orientation. Managers frequently derive "their" solution to a problem and then try to "sell" it to some colleagues and bypass or sandbag others in the commitment-building process. Too often, leaders, their team, and consultants fail to identify and tackle the adaptive dimensions of the challenge and to ask themselves, Who needs to learn what to develop, understand, commit to, and implement the strategy?

The same technical orientation entraps restructuring and business-process-reengineering initiatives, in which consultants and managers have the know-how to do the technical work of framing the objectives, designing a new work flow, documenting and communicating results, and identifying the activities to be performed by people in the organization. In many instances, reengineering falls short of the mark because it treats process redesign as a technical problem: managers neglect to identify the adaptive work and involve the people who have to do the changing. Senior executives fail to invest their time and their soul in understanding these issues and guiding people through the transition. Indeed, *engineering* is itself the wrong metaphor.

In short, the prevailing notion that leadership consists of having a vision and aligning people with that vision is bankrupt because it continues to treat adaptive situations as if they were technical: the authority figure is supposed to divine where the company is going, and people are supposed to follow. Leadership is reduced to a combination of grand knowing and salesmanship. Such a perspective reveals a basic misconception about the way businesses succeed in addressing adaptive challenges. Adaptive situations are hard to define and resolve precisely because they demand the work and responsibility of managers and people throughout the organization. They are not amenable to solutions provided by leaders; adaptive solutions require members of the organization to take responsibility for the problematic situations that face them.

Leadership has to take place every day. It cannot be the responsibility of the few, a rare event, or a once-in-a-lifetime opportunity. In our world, in our businesses, we face adaptive challenges all the time. When an executive is asked to square conflicting aspirations, he and his people face an adaptive challenge. When a manager sees a solution to a problem—technical in many respects except that it requires a change in the attitudes and habits of subordinates—she faces an adaptive challenge.

When an employee close to the front line sees a gap between the organization's purpose and the objectives he is asked to achieve, he faces both an adaptive challenge and the risks and opportunity of leading from below.

Leadership, as seen in this light, requires a learning strategy. A leader, from above or below, with or without authority, has to engage people in confronting the challenge, adjusting their values, changing perspectives, and learning new habits. To an authoritative person who prides himself on his ability to tackle hard problems, this shift may come as a rude awakening. But it also should ease the burden of having to know all the answers and bear all the load. To the person who waits to receive either the coach's call or "the vision" to lead, this change may also seem a mixture of good news and bad news. The adaptive demands of our time require leaders who take responsibility without waiting for revelation or request. One can lead with no more than a question in hand.

Originally published in January–February 1997
Reprint 97106

This article is based in part on Donald Heifetz's Leadership without Easy Answers *(Belknap Press of Harvard University Press, 1994).*

Whatever Happened to the Take-Charge Manager?

NITIN NOHRIA AND JAMES D. BERKLEY

Executive Summary

IN THE 1980S, U.S. business experienced an explosion of new managerial concepts unparalleled in previous decades. Management schools, consultants, and gurus all offered their own special formulas for how to stay competitive in increasingly challenging marketplaces.

Many American managers felt that the emergence of new managerial ideas signaled a rejuvenation of U.S. business. By readily adopting innovations like total quality programs and self-managed teams, managers believed they were demonstrating the kind of decisive leadership that kept companies competitive. But their thinking doesn't jibe with the facts. American managers did not take charge in the 1980s. Instead, they abdicated their responsibility to a burgeoning industry of management professionals.

Furthermore, the management fads of the last 15 years rarely produced their promised results. Between 1980 and 1990, market share in most key U.S. industries declined as much or more than it had in the 1970s.

If business leaders want to reverse this trend, they must reclaim managerial responsibility—and pragmatism is the place to start. Pragmatic managers are sensitive to their company's context and open to uncertainty. They focus on outcomes and are willing to make do. Pragmatic managers also avoid three common pitfalls, the "let's do it better this time" syndrome and the "flavor of the month" and "let's go for it all" approaches.

MANY MANAGERS FELT THAT THE EMERGENCE OF NEW MANAGERIAL IDEAS during the 1980s signaled the rejuvenation of U.S. business. By readily adopting innovations such as total quality programs and self-managed teams, managers believed that they were demonstrating the kind of decisive leadership that kept companies competitive. But such thinking doesn't jibe with the facts. American managers did not take charge in the 1980s. Instead, they abdicated their responsibility to a burgeoning industry of management professionals.

The 1980s witnessed the spectacular rise of management schools, consultants, media, and gurus who fed on the insecurities of American managers fearful of foreign competition and economic decline. (See the exhibit "The Rise of the Management Industry.") Mistrustful of their own judgment, many managers latched on to these

In the change-driven 1980s, the worst thing you could do was stick with the status quo.

self-appointed pundits, readily adopting their latest panaceas. Off-the-shelf programs addressing quality, customer satisfaction, time-to-market, strategic focus, core competencies, alliances, global competitiveness, organizational culture, and empowerment swept through U.S. corporations with alarming speed.

Adopting "new" ideas became a way for companies to signal to the world that they were progressive, that they had come to grips with their misguided pasts, and that they were committed to change. After all, the worst thing one could do was stick with the status quo.

For some businesses, the new ideas worked. They enabled companies to stem decline and challenge their

The Rise of the Management Industry

	1982	1992	Growth
Management Schools and MBAs			
Number of management schools	545	670	23%
Number of MBAs granted	60,000	80,000	33
Consulting Industry			
Number of consulting firms	780	1,533	97
Number of consultants	30,000	81,000	170
Total consulting revenues	$3.5 billion	$15.2 billion	334
Corporate Training			
Number of people trained	33.5 million	40.9 million	22
Total traing hours	1.1 billion	1.3 billion	18
Total corporate expenditures	$10 billion	$45 billion	350
Business Media			
Number of business stories	125,000	680,000	444
Number of new business books	1,327	1,831	38
Sales of business books	$225 million	$490 million	118

Source: *Authors' estimates, drawn from multiple sources. The authors gratefully acknowedge the assistance of Michael Stevenson and George Jenkins, both business information analysts at the Harvard Business School, in compiling these data.*

foreign competitors. But in the majority of cases, research shows, the management fads of the last 15 years rarely produced the promised results.

Between 1980 and 1990, market share in most key U.S. industries declined as much as or more than it had between 1970 and 1980. (See the exhibit "The Competitive Decline of U.S. Businesses.") Recent surveys at the Harvard Business School, McKinsey & Company, and Ernst & Young and the American Quality Foundation suggest that managers themselves are dissatisfied with the new management programs. In a study we conducted in 1993 at the Harvard Business School, we polled managers at nearly 100 companies on more than 21 different programs and found 75% of them to be unhappy with the results in their organizations.

The Competitive Decline of U.S. Businesses

U.S. Share as Percentage of Worldwide Sales of the 12 Largest Companies in Each Industry

Industry	1960	1970	1980	1990
Autos	83%	66%	42%	38%
Banking	61	67	26	0
Chemicals	68	40	31	23
Computers	95	90	86	70
Electricals	71	59	44	11
Iron and Steel	74	31	26	12
Textiles	58	44	41	21

Source: *Lawrence G. Franko, "Global Corporate Competition: Is the Large American Firm an Endangered Species?"* Business Horizons, November–December 1991. Reprinted with permission of the publisher.

What accounts for such disastrous results? We believe it is the failure of U.S. management to address its most serious problem: a lack of pragmatic judgment.

The manager's job is not to seek out novelty but to make sure the company gets results.

The widespread adoption of trendy management techniques during the 1980s allowed managers to rely on ready-made answers instead of searching for creative solutions. Although some companies are starting to question this reliance on quick fixes, the adoption of off-the-shelf "innovations" continues at a disturbing rate.

If managers want to reverse this trend, they must start by reclaiming managerial responsibility. Instead of subscribing impulsively to fads, they must pick and choose carefully the managerial ideas that promise to be useful. And they must adapt those ideas rigorously to the context of their companies.

Managers will often profit most by resisting new ideas entirely and making do with the materials at hand. However unfashionable this may seem, it is precisely as it should be. The manager's job is not to seek out novelty; it is to make sure the company gets results. Pragmatism is the place to start.

"Flavor of the Month" Managing

Given that managerial innovations disappoint with such regularity, we are surprised that companies continue to adopt them with such abandon. The lure of new management fads remains irresistible to managers looking for easy answers. And some companies seem particularly vulnerable to the gurus' hype.

We have identified three basic syndromes that perpetuate the adoption of ineffective, off-the-shelf solutions. The first might be called the "we didn't get it right
the first time, let's do it better this time" syndrome. In
this case, managers attribute the failure of an imported
practice or concept to some missing element in how the
idea was formulated and implemented. Old management consultants and champions are thrown out, and
new ones are brought in. Eager to succeed where others
have failed, the new pundits introduce variations on the
original idea that promise to set things right.

Unfortunately, in most cases, this syndrome has led
only to a proliferation of ideas, each one claiming—with
little justification—to be the correct one. Consider, for
example, today's increasingly fuzzy notion of total quality management (TQM). The Ernst & Young and American Quality Foundation study surveyed 584 companies
and found they used a total of 945 standardized programs, each promoted by different "experts."[1] In such an
environment, managers find themselves adrift in a sea of
competing ideas, increasingly insecure about whether
the right approach will ever be found.

Frustration with this all-too-common scenario leads
to a second pattern, which we term the "flavor of the
month" syndrome. In this scenario, managers cast aside
old ideas as misguided and introduce new ones that will
finally—this time—deliver the business to the promised
land. Thus, for instance, TQM programs are derided for
their incremental nature, while reengineering is champi-
oned as the key to achieving "breakthrough" performance. The half-life of such ideas is becoming so short
that we find managers shifting abruptly from one idea to
the next. Employees wise up to this syndrome very
quickly. Experience teaches them not to get terribly

enthused about any new idea. They learn to shrug it off, reasoning, "If we wait until Monday, this too shall pass."

Other companies fall into a third syndrome: they "go for it all." We know of one large U.S. bank where the vice president of HR proudly declared that his organization had implemented every new management program it could find. It had more than 1,000 self-managed teams, over 500 quality initiatives, more than 300 reengineering initiatives, and a host of other programs. Of course, if you probed a bit, you discovered that the majority of these initiatives addressed such crucial management issues as what color to paint the walls. Employees found all their time taken up participating in initiatives of varying importance. And this was happening in an organization where the core business was eroding at an alarming rate.

What happens when managers or their gurus are confronted with the situations we have been depicting? In our experience, they tend to respond with a few unchallengeable replies: "It's only natural to expect some failures—look at the great successes that other companies have had"; "It's not easy to change decades of existing practice"; or, "In time, we'll see results." By deflecting all possibility of judgment into the future like this, it is possible to sustain faith in a managerial promised land almost indefinitely.

But what about the success stories of the new management? Certainly, there have been some, but they have happened because managers used their ingenuity to adapt new ideas, such as TQM, to the particular contexts of their companies. When tailored to fit specific situations, and often changed beyond recognition, these new ideas can prove invaluable. This is pragmatic management at its best.

The Four Faces of Pragmatism

We are calling for a return to pragmatism as espoused by the nineteenth-century American pragmatists: to judge any idea by its practical consequences, by seeing what it allows you to do, rather than by chasing after an elusive notion of truth. Or as the pragmatist philosopher William James put it, "Theories are instruments, not answers to enigmas in which we can rest." Every managerial situation, we believe, demands a pragmatic attitude. For purposes of discussion, we can divide this approach into four general components: sensitivity to context, willingness to make do, focus on outcomes, and openness to uncertainty.

Sensitivity to context. We cannot stress enough that the central concept of pragmatic management is the need to adapt ideas to a given context. Being able to judge the parameters of a particular situation and decide what ideas and actions will work in that context is what distinguishes the truly effective manager. (See "Double-Edged Pragmatist: An Interview with Shikhar Ghosh" on page 217.)

Context includes both the macro and micro—from the cultural milieu of a host country, for example, to the personalities of employees on a management team. Managers who are sensitive to context have a keen sense of the company's history, including the successes and failures of past management programs. They know the company's resources intimately, from physical assets to human capital. And they understand the organization's and the employees' strengths and weaknesses, so they can discern what actions are possible and how much the organization can be stretched.

Pragmatic managers understand that a change initiative that worked in one context could just as easily fail in another and that programs must be continually reevaluated as circumstances evolve. Otherwise, change programs can get stuck at lofty levels of abstraction and ambiguity and have little relevance to the day-to-day workings of the corporation. Even when an overall program like TQM has been adopted, managers should make frequent pragmatic judgments about how best to implement it. Management gurus may peddle a glossary of rules that describe how to do this, but universal answers rarely meet particular needs.

Many successful management innovations have come from companies that have adapted, not adopted, popular ideas.

Many of the most successful managerial innovations in recent years have come from companies that have adapted, rather than adopted, popular ideas. Consider an example that has been much in the news in recent years, GE's Work-Out program.[2] Before developing Work-Out in the late 1980s, GE tried to implement the popular Japanese quality circles, teams of employees dedicated to significant quality improvement, throughout the company.

In Japanese quality circles, people are isolated in small groups that often receive substantial direction from above. This approach, GE soon discovered, had limited value in an American context, however. CEO Jack Welch believed the top-down model would never foster the trust necessary to convince line employees to buy into major change. Nor would it sway many middle and upper level managers, whom he saw as "actively resistant to new ideas."

In 1989, Welch began replacing quality circles with the broader, homespun Work-Out program. Instead of gathering in small groups, workers and managers met in large forums dedicated to airing new ideas, the more radical the better. Frequency and duration of work-outs were flexible, according to need, and the town-meeting-like settings fostered a sense of community while ensuring the visibility of individual contributions. The public setting also forced reticent managers to face up to pressures for change. Welch insisted that managers give on-the-spot responses to employee proposals. Nothing was considered sacred in the Work-Out program. Even major changes like overhauling an existing business process (now hyped as reengineering) could be brought up and dealt with in less than a day. In sum, by following the pragmatic strategy of tailoring a program to fit the company, GE was able to avoid the pitfalls of generic quality management.

By tailoring a program to the company, GE avoided the pitfalls of quality management.

Homespun solutions are not always the answer, however. Sometimes it makes the most sense for companies to abandon ideas entirely, even those touted as "the next big thing." Some companies have discovered, for example, that just-in-time manufacturing, while beautiful theoretically, doesn't make sense in their manufacturing contexts. Even some Japanese companies that use JIT at home have found that American marketing methods and distribution systems make JIT less attractive in the United States.

Even the best management ideas have had a half-life of no more than 10 to 15 years.

In stressing the importance of sensitivity to context, however, we are not advocating a rejection of any idea that originates outside the company. We would hate to see managers conclude too quickly, "It won't work because our context is so different." That will stop the flow of ideas. We are urging only that innovative ideas, such as TQM, and basic management practices, such as strategic planning, be adopted with an acute sensitivity to the situation at hand. Careful forethought and monitoring should determine how practices are used and to what extent they are followed. Managers should also bear in mind that a solution that works today may fail tomorrow. After all, even the best management ideas, such as portfolio planning, have had a half-life of no more than 10 to 15 years.

Willingness to make do. Pragmatic managers, we have found, are particularly adept at "making do." They know what resources are available and how to round up more on short notice; they seek pragmatic answers based on the materials at hand.

We call this aspect of pragmatism *bricolage*, a word French anthropologist Claude Lévi-Strauss used to describe the thought processes of primitive societies.

Effective managers play with possibilities, tinker with systems, and use all their resources to find workable solutions.

Against prevailing stereotypes of these societies as intellectually inferior, Lévi-Strauss argued that they have ingenious, nonrational ways of thinking. They reason inductively, deriving principles from their daily experience to guide them. For example, these societies have developed elaborate systems of medicine by continually experimenting with local herbs and flowers until they discover the right mixtures to cure their ailments.

Effective managers are *bricoleurs* in this same sense. They play with possibilities and use available resources to find workable solutions. They tinker with systems and variables, constantly on the lookout for improved configurations.

One of our favorite examples of bricolage comes from a director we met a few years ago at a large telecommunications company. While most other people were focusing on the massive IT overhaul the company needed, she directed her attention to how it could use the existing computer resources more creatively.

The engineers who maintained the huge telecommunications network stored data on a trio of aging, overstuffed, and incompatible mainframes. Most people believed it was time to scrap them and install a new, cutting-edge information architecture that would integrate all the company's computer resources. The director concurred that the mainframes would eventually have to go, but she believed it didn't have to happen right away, and, given the time necessary for planning such a change, it couldn't. Why not get the most we can from the mainframes in the interim, she asked. Why not use computer workstations to simulate the multimillion-dollar information architecture that the company would have in the future? With little direction from above, she and her team developed a series of software applications that delayed the need for mainframe replacement while, at the same time, cutting the system-project time from months to weeks.

When a bricoleur is making do, solutions are never fixed or final. This innovative director's project evolved constantly from the day it was conceived until it was sent on-line. Indeed, being a bricoleur entails a willingness to take actions without a clear sense of how things are going to unfold in the future. This doesn't mean that bricoleurs don't care about results, but that they are willing to experiment to get there.

Motorola CEO Bob Galvin's skillful management of a change effort during the 1980s is another good example of bricolage. In 1983, Motorola had just come off a very good year, but Galvin was aware of rumblings throughout the company that the organizational structure wasn't working because it was too bureaucratic. A recent trip to Japan had also convinced him that Motorola was slow to respond to changes in the marketplace.

Rather than waiting for a crisis to erupt, postponing action until he could come up with the perfect strategy, or hiring outside consultants to implement a prepackaged program, Galvin plunged his managers into the change process. At a May meeting of more than 100 senior officers, he announced that the corporation would begin a large-scale change initiative. What he neglected to say was how.

Understandably, the officers were confused. No one was clear about the CEO's agenda or what anyone was expected to do. And this is precisely what Galvin was after. He wanted the officers to be creative and to experiment with different ways of addressing the problems they were confronting in their particular situations. While some managers became preoccupied with "not really knowing what Galvin wanted," others used his challenge as a jumping-off point for experimentation. They came up with numerous structural changes and product innovations, from more market-driven business units to a new line of cellular products, which enabled Motorola to weather an economic downturn and emerge as the most powerful player in the cellular industry. An intuitive pragmatist, Galvin had created a situation that allowed those closest to the problems to come up with solutions.

Focus on outcomes. Pragmatists are concerned with getting results. But they don't get overly hung up on how to get them. The telecommunications director didn't mind a Rube Goldberg approach to system design if it could make a positive contribution to the business. The managers who rejected just-in-time manufacturing realized that the most elegant theory would mean nothing if it couldn't improve delivery time.

Failure to focus on outcomes can spell disaster. Consider the case of the large bank we referred to earlier that had "gone for it all," adopting every change program in the book. Progress was defined in terms of the number of people who had received quality training and the number of quality and reengineering teams that had been established. This had created the illusion of progress. But the bank's performance continued to decline.

Allen-Bradley, a Rockwell-owned manufacturer of industrial controls, learned the hard way about the value of focusing on outcomes. The company's early experience with team-based management at its Industrial Computer and Communications Group had been successful because the teams had a clear mission: to deliver an innovative computer-integrated manufacturing product as quickly as possible. Their focus on outcomes made them flexible and pragmatic; when it was more reasonable for a few people to tackle a problem instead of a team, they went off on their own and did it.

When ICCG switched the whole organization to teams, however, the mission became more diffuse. Teams became a virtue unto themselves, and suddenly all problems had to be solved through teams, whether or not this was the most pragmatic solution. People became caught up in the novelty of teams, and the company took on a summer-camp atmosphere. "Whoever dies with the most teams wins," an employee joked.

Eventually, senior managers noticed that the proliferation of teams had led to a lack of discipline, while failing to get rid of the negative bureaucratic elements of the old system. Chastened by this experience, ICCG began using teams much more cautiously. Today senior managers decide when, where, and how teams are used. First, they ask three critical questions: Is a team necessary? What will we gain? How will we measure our gains? The emphasis is less on fostering camaraderie than on seeing concrete results.

An incident at a major computer company shows what happens when a manager focuses on the wrong outcome. After years of indifferent performance, the company's PC division was finally beginning to show some signs of life. The hardware group had developed a full line of PCs that could compete on price. A third-party software group had made promising alliances with major software vendors. And an internal software development group had produced a networking product that had great market potential.

To promote these new products, the managers of each group asked the division's marketing director to assign additional people to their marketing efforts. Had this director been thinking pragmatically, she might have assigned a couple of key staff members to each group. But she refused because she did not want to take the focus off her first priority, improving the performance of her overall marketing department.

With this goal in mind, she hired internal and external consultants to initiate a formal strategic planning exercise. To empower her people and maintain a spirit of participation, she solicited input at a series of off-site meetings and undertook team-building exercises. Of course, while all this was going on, the three managers felt like Nero was fiddling while Rome burned. Eventually, they appealed to the division's vice president, who intervened and broke up the marketing department. He assigned the director's star employees to the three groups and left her with only a skeletal staff. The marketing director had become so caught up in developing a trendy new strategy for her department that she had lost sight of the outcomes critical to her company's success. And she lost her employees in the process.

An important part of pragmatism is the willingness to embrace uncertainty and surprise.

Openness to uncertainty. The last important component of a pragmatic attitude is a willingness to embrace uncertainty and surprise. We believe that most of today's off-the-shelf managerial innovations foster a regimentation that discourages managers from dealing effectively with the unexpected. The fashionable emphasis on being "proactive" can give a false sense that all circumstances can be anticipated. But more often than not, managers are thrown into situations in which they must act quickly and without certainty. To quote economist Kenneth Arrow, in many situations, "we must simply act, fully knowing our ignorance of possible consequences."

For those who associate pragmatism with conservatism or prudence, stressing an openness to uncertainty may seem counterintuitive. But the two concepts are linked. Pragmatists understand that it is unrealistic to try to avoid uncertainty. Attempts to deny or ignore it can blind managers to the real contexts in which they are working and prevent them from responding effectively. Instead of fearing sudden changes, pragmatic managers welcome them as unanticipated opportunities. They learn to capitalize on the unexpected, whether implementing a companywide change initiative or making a critical business decision. (See "Pragmatism in an Age of Ready-Made Answers" on page 222.)

Reebok CEO Paul Fireman is a manager who knows how to profit from uncertainty. At a shoe manufacturers' show in Europe in 1989, Fireman was unimpressed by the merchandise displayed on the floor. He noticed that members of the trade press, looking for a good story, seemed bored with the show as well. Fireman realized that this situation presented an opportunity for Reebok; if he could come up with something new and exciting, he could generate a lot of publicity. A Reebok

The marketing plan wasn't finished, but Reebok launched THE PUMP anyway.

product that was still in development, THE PUMP, boasted an innovative, inflatable technology that could give the wearer a close personal fit. He knew it would make a great story. But the marketing plan for the shoe had not been completed, and many details had not been worked out, including the price. But Fireman decided to "just do it." He introduced THE PUMP at the show.

The early launch turned out to be a hit. These rave

reviews, according to Fireman, not only created market anticipation for the shoe but also helped "light a fire inside the company to get the product developed and released quickly." It was produced in record time and turned out to be a huge success in the marketplace.

Fireman's boldness could have gotten the company in trouble had Reebok not been able to deliver on time. Many companies have been skewered in the press for making new product promises they couldn't keep. But Fireman's move was not quite as brash as it seemed. He based it on a quick but careful assessment of the state of the industry, his company's capabilities, and just how much Reebok could be stretched in a pinch. Because he understood the context in which he was operating, Fireman was able to seize the moment. No time-to-market program could have produced such positive results. No companywide initiative can ever be a substitute for the pragmatic judgment of an individual manager.

AMERICAN MANAGEMENT IS AT A CROSSROADS. It must decide whether to continue on its present path, on the fruitless quest for managerial Holy Grails, or whether to face up to the challenge of pragmatism. It is worth noting that in many academic disciplines, this sort of pragmatism has witnessed something of a revival. American management may stand to gain the most from looking back to this indigenous style of thought, particularly to its pragmatic successes of the past.

The best managers have always know how to create urgency with or without a new management paradigm.

A case in point is the long list of uncommon accomplishments of the United States during World War II. Planes were designed, built, and flown safely in combat in less than two years. Today it takes more than ten years to accomplish the same. During the war, ships were built in weeks; today it takes years. And one could go on and on with stories of achievements that now seem beyond the realm of possibility. A crisis like World War II focuses people on pragmatic action in an uncommon way. It unites national and personal interests. Of course, it may be nearly impossible to replicate such conditions, but creating this kind of urgency is exactly what effective managers have always known how to do. And they have always been able to create urgency with or without the invocation of a brand-new management paradigm.

We are by no means arguing that the new ideas hyped to managers are without worth or that managers should go back to focusing on the much-maligned bureaucratic practices of the past. Instead, we are saying that the time has come to reconsider the relative balance between management innovations and management fundamentals. If the eighties were the time for the flowering of new perspectives on managerial practice, the remainder of the nineties may be the time for a sober reevaluation of managerial responsibility.

Double-Edged Pragmatist: An Interview with Shikhar Ghosh

Shikhar Ghosh was a partner at the Boston Consulting Group, specializing in creating responsive organizations until 1988, when he became CEO of the Appex Corpo-

ration, a start-up cellular communications company. Now called EDS Personal Communications Corporation and a division of Electronic Data Systems, it is an $8 billion business and one of the fastest growing information management enterprises.

A self-avowed pragmatist, Ghosh speaks about his experience as an outsider who has recommended change strategies to corporations and as a CEO who implements change from within. He also discusses his role as a bricoleur, a pragmatic manager who constantly tinkers with systems and variables to create a stronger organization.

How would you define pragmatism as it relates to organizational change programs?

Being pragmatic is creating a balance between a company's objectives and constraints. The constraints may be its finances, history, relationships, or employees' ability to learn. You have to adjust constantly the objectives of any change program to conform to what a company can learn and absorb.

Do any organizational change fads you've seen live up to the hype?

Many have merit, but they often represent only particular truths. When you combine these change fads with the reality of a company, you get very mixed results. Quality and reengineering are not bad in themselves, but management gurus underplay the practical difficulty of implementing them in an organization. Gurus represent these programs as complete solutions, when most of them deal with only one facet of an organization's problems.

Most programs view companies as machines. But companies are more like organisms. If you do something to them, they react. And a program has to be fine-tuned constantly based on those reactions.

What kind of organizational problems did you encounter at Appex?

Appex had no structure. When I arrived, I called a meeting of the 25 employees to say that we needed some rules. I said that people had to be in by 10 A.M., or they had to call in. Someone got up and said, "What right do you have to tell us anything?"

So what did you do?

I implemented a Japanese circular structure to instill discipline without losing informality or building in too much hierarchy. I was in the center of the organizational chart, and groups were around me in concentric circles. People doing different functions were at the same level, and the boundaries between groups were blurred. For example, customer service flowed into engineering; engineering flowed into marketing.

The structure was based on Japanese principles of flat organizations, but we didn't just pull it out of a textbook. We designed the structure pragmatically to reflect the way people really worked.

How did it work?

We found that we could respond very quickly to changes in the market. And we were far more innovative than many competitors. But in a short while, we realized that we were growing too rapidly to allow for this level of informal communication. There was no standardized way of doing things. If work didn't get done, no one knew who was accountable.

What happened next?

Within six months, we went to the other extreme and opted for a functional organization. Department managers reported to me, and lower level managers reported to them. To some extent, this went against the grain. But by this time, employees saw the need for more structure. We were missing deadlines. Too much work was falling between the cracks.

Choosing a functional organization was initially a pragmatic move in that it addressed an urgent problem: the need for procedures and accountability. Within a few months, however, Appex developed the traditional symptoms of bureaucracy: lack of flexibility and responsiveness. There was no teamwork, and people started to align themselves more with their functions than with overall company goals.

And the next move?

Teams. People served on cross-functional teams that focused on one line of the business. This approach worked reasonably well for seven months, until we realized that we had too many products and not enough general management talent to direct all the teams.

So we restructured the company, tailoring the team concept to our own constraints. We consolidated the teams so that each one handled several lines of work. And we turned them into self-contained divisions. Traditional wisdom said we were too small to divide the company, but because of our needs and limitations, it was the pragmatic choice for us.

Were your employees starting to feel dizzy from all these changes?

In the beginning, employees would say, "Wait, not another structure!"

But then they got used to change and saw its value. After a while, an organizational structure becomes a tool you're using to create a balance between conflicting modes of organizational behavior, such as flexibility and consistency. Each structure emphasizes one type of behavior and deemphasizes another. By continuing to change, you can balance the needs of the organization.

Some of what is learned from an organizational change program stays with employees long after the program is replaced. People get to know one another; they understand other functions. And because the organization is constantly changing, people don't have time to develop a power base within a particular structure. They have to identify with the broader objectives of the company.

So, are you a bricoleur?

Yes, I guess I am. While it seems as if we implemented changes every six months, in reality, we were constantly changing. We weren't satisfied with off-the-shelf solutions. We were always tweaking the structure we had in place. And when we bumped against too many constraints, we would change the structure once again.

When you change often, you know that nothing is permanent. You don't have to have all the answers before you try something. You can afford to experiment because the current structure doesn't have to be "just right."

Managing is a matter of constantly looking at the way you do things and adjusting the process to reflect your goals and resources.That's pragmatism. You use the resources you have to get where you need to go.

—Julia Lieblich

Pragmatism in an Age of Ready-Made Answers

MANAGEMENT IDEAS SHOULD BE:

- Adopted only after careful consideration
- Purged of unnecessary buzzwords and clichés
- Judged by their practical consequences
- Tied to the here and now
- Rooted in genuine problems
- Adapted to suit particular people and circumstances
- Adaptable to changing and unforeseen conditions
- Tested and refined through active experimentation
- Discarded when they are no longer useful

Notes

1. "The International Quality Study—Best Practices Report" (Cleveland, Ohio: American Quality Foundation and Ernst & Young, 1992).

2. Work-Out is discussed in detail in Noel M. Tichy and Stratford Sherman, *Control Your Destiny or Someone Else Will: How Jack Welch Is Making G.E. the World's Most Competitive Corporation* (New York: Doubleday, 1993).

Originally published in January–February 1994
Reprint 94109

About the Contributors

JOSEPH L. BADARACCO, JR. is the John Shad Professor of Business Ethics at Harvard Business School and a member of the School's general management unit. He has taught courses on strategy, general management, business-government relations, and business ethics in the School's MBA and executive programs. He currently serves as chairman of Harvard University's Advisory Committee on Shareholder Responsibility. His most recent books, *Business Ethics: Roles and Responsibilities* and *Defining Moments: When Managers Must Choose Between Right and Wrong* (HBS Press, 1997), have been translated into eight languages.

JAMES D. BERKLEY is currently a Ph.D. student in comparative literature at the University of California, Los Angeles. Between 1990 and 1994, he worked as a research associate and case writer in organizational behavior at the Harvard Business School, where he helped co-write *Beyond the Hype: Rediscovering the Essence of Management* with Professors Nitin Nohria and Robert G. Eccles. Both at Harvard and UCLA, his main research interests have involved the interrelations between science, literature, and society and the intellectual currents of the later nineteenth and twentieth centuries.

CHARLES FARKAS is the director of Bain & Company. He advises chief executives and top level managers in a wide variety of industries on issues critical to long-term success. Mr.

Farkas is currently the head of Bain & Company's Global
Financial Services Practice. He has also been a leader in the
areas of health care, consumer products, retailing, and manufacturing and still spends part of his time working with
clients in these areas. Mr. Farkas is the author of the best-
selling book *Maximum Leadership* and numerous articles in
the *Harvard Business Review*, *Fortune*, and other publications.

RONALD A. HEIFETZ directs the Leadership Education
Project at Harvard University's John F. Kennedy School of
Government. For the last fourteen years, he has been responsible for developing a theory of leadership and a method of
leadership development. His research aims to provide strategy
and tactics for mobilizing adaptive work in politics, businesses, and nonprofits. Formerly the director of Cor Associates, a
research and development group, and clinical instructor in
psychiatry at Harvard Medical School, Mr. Heifetz works
extensively with leaders in government and industry. He is
the author of the widely acclaimed book *Leadership Without
Easy Answers* (The Belknap/Harvard University Press, 1994).

JOHN P. KOTTER is the Konosuke Matsushita Professor of
Leadership at the Harvard Business School. He is the author
of seven best selling business books, including most recently
Leading Change (HBS Press, 1996). He has also created two
highly acclaimed executive videos, one on *Leadership* (1991),
and one on *Corporate Culture* (1993). The many honors won
by Professor Kotter include an Exxon Award for Innovation in
Graduate Business School Curriculum Design, a Johnson,
Smith & Knisely Award for New Perspectives in Business
Leadership, and a McKinsey Award for best *Harvard Business
Review* article. He is widely regarded as the best speaker in the
world on topics of leadership and change.

DONALD L. LAURIE is the founder and managing director of
the management consulting firm Laurie International Limit-

ed. His work focuses on strategic management issues relevant
to chairmen and chief executives. His corporate assignments
have been with clients concerned with crafting strategic
architecture, managing change, and improving the quality of
leadership. Mr. Laurie's ongoing research, *The Work of the
Leader* (1998), involves chief executives of major corporations
and has received wide acclaim by business leaders in the U.S.
and Europe.

HENRY MINTZBERG jointly holds the positions of Cleghorn
Professor of Management Studies at McGill University in
Montreal, Canada and Professor of Organization at INSEAD
in Fontainebleau, France. His research deals with issues of
general management and organizations, currently focusing on
the nature and styles of managerial work, as well as continuing work on forms of organizing and on the strategy formation process. He is the author of ninety articles and seven
books, including most recently *The Canadian Condition:
Reflections of a "Pure Cotton"* (1995).

NITIN NOHRIA is a professor of business administration at
the Harvard Business School. His research interests center on
leadership and corporate renewal. The author of five books,
his most recent, *The Differentiated Network,* provides an innovative model for organizing multinational corporations. Professor Nohria is currently investigating the dynamics of
organizational change through a series of projects that study
the impact on Fortune 100 companies of corporate downsiz-
ing, the spread of strategic alliances, total quality management, and tighter corporate governance.

THOMAS TEAL was at the *Harvard Business Review* for eight
years, and is now a senior editor at the Boston Consulting
Group, an international consulting firm headquartered in
Boston. His previous experience includes five years at *The
New Yorker* magazine, two years as managing editor of the

White House speechwriting office under President Carter, two decades as a translator of Swedish, Danish, and Norwegian, and in the early 1960's, one year as a night secretary to comedian Lenny Bruce. "The Human Side of Management" is adapted from his introduction to *First Person: Tales of Management Courage and Tenacity* (HBS Press, 1996).

SUZY WETLAUFER, formerly of the international management consulting firm Bain & Company, is a senior editor of the *Harvard Business Review*, specializing in the area of organization. In addition to "The Team That Wasn't," she is the author of several *HBR* pieces, including "What's Killing the Creativity at Coolburst?" and, with Harvard Business School's David Thomas, "A Question of Color."

ABRAHAM ZALEZNIK is the Konosuke Matsushita Professor of Leadership, Emeritus at the Harvard Business School. He is known internationally for his research and teaching in the field of social psychology in the business setting, and for his investigations into the distinguishing characteristics in leadership and the psychological aspects of executive behavior of managers and leaders. He has published fourteen books, the latest being *Learning Leadership* (1993), and has written numerous award winning articles. He is chairman of the board of King Ranch and a member of the board of Ogden Corporations, Timberland Co., Freedom Communications, Inc., and Butchers, Inc., He is a consultant to businesses, corporations, and government.

Index

abortion, 106–111, 112
adaptive work, 172–197. *See
    also* work
    decentralization of respon-
        sibility and, 183–185
    defined, 173
    disciplined attention and,
        181–183
    identification of challenges
        and, 176–178
    at KPMG Netherlands,
        187–194
    leadership as learning and,
        194–197
    leadership from below and,
        183–187
    perspective and, 172–176,
        188
    regulation of distress and,
        178–181
Adario, Peter (pseudonym),
    99–104, 111
Akers, John, 85
aligning people, as managerial
    role, 41, 44–47, 56–58
Allen-Bradley (company),
    212–213, 214

American Express, 53–55
American Quality Foundation,
    204
Anglo American (South
    African company), 130,
    132
Appex Corporation, 217–218,
    219–221
Aristotle, 93
Arrow, Kenneth, 214–215
asbestos crisis at Johns-
    Manville, 154–156
attention, disciplined, 181–183
auditing, as control system, 134
authority, delegation of, 23,
    118–119, 158, 160–161
automotive industry, 84
autonomy, 189
AXA Group (French company),
    136
AXAnetics (invented lan-
    guage), 136

Baluieu, Etienne-Emile, 110
BankAmerica, 136, 144
Bébéar, Claude, 135–136
Beers, Charlotte, 130, 132

Bolduc, J. P., 140
Bond, John, 134–135
Both, Hennie, 190, 191
"box approach" to leadership, 120, 133–137, 144
bricolage (anthropological concept), 209–211, 218, 221
British Airways, 136–137, 176–178, 179
broadening, and leadership, 50–51
Burns, James MacGregor, 87

Calloway, Wayne, 127
Carlson, Sune, 28
Carlzon, Jan, 43, 182, 184–185
Carnegie, Andrew, 80
Cattabiani, Gene, 167–169
CEOs. *See also* executives; leadership; management; managers
    "box approach" and, 120, 133–137, 144
    change approach and, 120–121, 137–142
    contacts of, 15
    development projects and, 18–19
    expertise approach and, 119–120, 130–132
    human-assets approach and, 119, 126–129, 133
    role of, 117, 142–143
    strategy approach and, 118–119, 122–126, 137
    travel and, 126–127

"cerebral face" of management, 30–32
challenge
    adaptive challenges and, 173–197
    leadership and, 50
change
    as approach to leadership, 120–121, 137–142
    barriers to, 148
    coping with, 40, 41, 42, 47–50, 139
    individual, 191
    "new ideas" and, 201
    pain of, 181
    pragmatism and, 207
    resistance to, 188–191
change agents, 139–141
chaos, conceptions of, 87
character, and managers, 90–112, 150–152
CinMade, 161–165
Cizik, Robert, 131–132
clarity, and control systems, 135
Coca-Cola, 124, 125
communication. *See also* information
    adaptive work and, 181, 186
    CEOs and, 126–127
    company newsletters and, 140
    at Eastman Kodak, 56
    indirect, 74
    informational roles of managers and, 16–18, 22
    trust and, 49

competition, in the 1980s, 202
complexity, coping with, 39–41, 125
computers
  travel industry and, 153
  work of managers and, 11
confidence, 193–194
conflict
  adaptive challenges and, 178
  avoidance of, 190
  management of, 180, 182–183
Connor, Fox, 79
consensus building, 140
"consulting engineers," 132
controlling, and management, 2, 41, 47–50, 160–161. *See also* delegation of authority
control systems, 47, 120, 133–137, 144
Cooper Industries, 131
core values, 91–92, 95–96, 108. *See also* values
courage, 150, 152
Crandall, Bob, 56–58
creativity. *See also* innovation
  adaptive work and, 194
  control systems and, 136–137
  strategy and, 191–192
credibility, 46
curiosity, 193
customers
  British Airways and, 176–178, 179

CEOs and, 123, 136–137
  managers and, 7
  vision and, 43

Daimler-Benz, 121–122
decentralization
  at Eastman Kodak, 56
  leadership and, 51
  at Scandinavian Airlines System, 184
decision-making role of managers, 18–21, 22
defining moments
  for executives, 105–111
  for individuals, 93–98
  managers and, 90–112
  for work groups, 98–104
delegation of authority, 23, 118–119, 158, 160–161. *See also* controlling, and management
Dell, Michael, 124–125
Dell Computer, 124–125
deregulation, and travel industry, 153–154
Dewey, John, 91
direction-setting, 41, 53–55, 180
discipline
  attention and, 181–183
  teams and, 213
disseminator, manager's role as, 17
distress, and adaptive work, 178–181
disturbance handler, manager's role as, 19

diversity, in organizations, 181,
182
Donner, Frederic G., 65
Du Pont, Pierre, 67, 68, 69

Eastman Kodak, 56–58
EDS Personal Communications
Corporation, 218
Einstein, Albert, 78
Eisenhower, Dwight D., 9, 28,
78–80
Electronic Data Systems, 218
employees
adaptive work and, 174
"company way" values and,
129
empowerment and, 46
fads in management and,
204, 205
hostile relations with,
162–164, 167–169
human-assets approach
and, 119, 126–129, 133
incentive programs and, 131
layoffs and, 156–158
motivation of, 14
responsibility and, 184
risk-taking among, 55, 138
treatment of, 158
vision and, 43, 48
Work-Out program and, 208
empowerment
aligning people and, 46–47
management and, 158–161
energy, and vision, 48
"engineers, consulting," 132

entrepreneurship
entrepreneurs as heroes
and, 166
environment at Proctor &
Gamble and, 60
managers and, 18
organizational culture and,
65
equilibrium, and adaptive
work, 181, 182, 184, 185
Ernst & Young, 204
esemplastic imagination, 152
ethical decisions, 90–112
Ethics (Aristotle), 93
*Executive Role Constellation,
The* (Hodgson, Levinson,
and Zaleznik), 29
executives. *See also* CEOs; leadership; management;
managers
adaptive work and, 173–174,
183
alignment of people and, 45
defining moments for,
105–111
expediency, and defining
moments, 96–98
expertise approach, 119–120,
130–132

family, and development of
leadership, 76–77
Fayol, Henri, 2, 3, 4
feelings, conflicted, 93–95
figurehead, manager as, 13
Fireman, Paul, 215–216

"flavor of the month" syndrome, 203–205
Ford Motor Company, 67
Fortis (Belgian company), 134
Frey, Robert, 161–165
Friedman, Stephen, 139–142, 145

Galvin, Robert, 131, 211–212
game theory, 73–74
General Electric, 51, 207–208
General Motors, 67–69
George, Peter, 122
Gerstner, Lou, 53–55
"getting on the balcony," 175–176, 188
Ghosh, Shikhar, 217–221
Gillette, 127, 128
goals, 65–67. *See also* vision
Goizueta, Roberto, 124, 125
Goldman Sachs, 139–140, 145
Guest, Robert H., 15, 28

Hanley, John W., 82
health, and adaptive work, 172–173
heroism, 166
Hewlett-Packard, 51
Hodgson, Richard C., 28–29
Hoechst (German company), 106, 111
holding environment, 179
Homans, George C., 16, 29
Hong Kong Shanghai Banking Company, 134–135

honor, 154
HSBC Holdings, 134–135
human-assets approach to leadership, 119, 126–129, 133
Human Group, The (Homans), 16, 29
human interactions, and managers, 150–169
Hunter, John, 124

IBM, 85
ICCG, 212–214
imagination, 152–154, 194. *See also* innovation
Industrial Computer and Communications Group (ICCG), 212–213, 214
informal networks, 49–50
information. *See also* communication
    control systems and, 134–135
    informational roles of managers and, 16–18, 22
    liaison role and, 22
    mail processing and, 8, 17
    management and, 5, 7–10, 11, 16–18, 22
    organizations and, 183–184
    processing of, 17
    sharing of, 23–24
    "soft," 9
    verbal, 10, 17, 23
innovation, 138, 148, 203–205, 207. *See also* imagination

In Search of Excellence (Peters and Waterman), 32
"insightful face" of management, 30–32
integrity, 150, 154–156
interdependence, 44–45
International Paper, 145
interpersonal roles of managers, 13–15, 16, 22

James, William, 75, 76, 101, 102, 206
Japan, 207–208, 219
JIT. *See* just-in-time manufacturing
Johns-Manville, 154–156
Johnson, Earvin ("Magic"), 175
Johnson & Johnson, 51, 154
Johnsonville Sausage, 160–161
junk bonds, 139–140
just-in-time manufacturing (JIT), 208–209, 212

Kelleher, Herb, 127–128, 129, 145
Kennedy, John F., 70
Kettering, Charles, 67–68, 69
Koedijk, Ruud, 187–191
KPMG Netherlands, 187–194

labor unions, 162, 164, 167–169
Ladbroke Group (British company), 122
Lance, Bert, 83
Land, Edwin, 66
language, as control system, 136

layoffs, 156–158
leadership. *See also* CEOs; executives; management; managers
adaptive work and, 172–197
approaches to, 116–146
"box approach" to, 120, 133–137, 144
broadening and, 50–51
CEOs approaches to, 116–146
change as approach to, 120–121, 137–142
collective, 62
conceptions of work and, 69–70
coping with change and, 40, 41, 42, 47–50
credibility and, 46
decentralization and, 51
defined, 38, 40, 64
development of, 50–53, 62–65, 76–83
as distinguished from management, 38–53, 62–87
emotional capacity and, 181
human-assets approach to, 119, 126–129, 133
as learning, 194–197
in the military, 40
personality and, 143–144, 145, 146
relations with others and, 73–74
research on, 116–146
self-confidence and, 185
sense of self and, 76

in sports, 175
strategy approach to,
    118–119, 122–126, 137
"voices from below" and,
    185–187
learning, leadership as,
    194–197
Levinson, Daniel J., 28–29
Lévi-Strauss, Claude, 209
Lewis, Steve (pseudonym),
    93–98, 111
liaison, manager's role as, 14,
    22
Lippens, Maurice, 134
long-term planning, 43–44
Lotus, 86

Machiavelli, Niccolò, 104
mail processing, 8, 17
management. *See also* CEOs;
    executives; leadership;
    managers
  aligning people and, 41,
    44–47, 56–58
  "cerebral face" of, 30–32
  computers and, 11
  controlling and, 2, 41,
    47–50, 160–161
  as coping with complexity,
    39–41
  at the crossroads, 216–217
  defined, 39–40, 63–64, 221
  difficulty of, 150
  direction-setting and, 41,
    53–55
  as distinguished from lead-
    ership, 38–53, 62–87

effective, 23–26, 206
empowerment and, 158–161
fads in, 200–217
game theory and, 73–74
greatness and, 150–169
heroism and, 166
imagination and, 152–154
inferior, 148–150
information and, 5, 7–10, 11,
    16–18, 22
innovation and, 138,
    203–205, 207
"insightful face" of, 30–32
integrity and, 150, 154–156
Japanese theories of,
    207–208, 219
long-term planning and,
    43–44
motivation and, 41, 58–60,
    165–166
myths about, 4–12
in the 1980s, 200–217
in the 19th century, 11
organizing and, 2, 41, 44–47
originality and, 152
planning and, 24–25, 41,
    42–45, 47
pragmatic, 203, 204–217
proactive, 214
research on, 27–29, 204
responsibility and, 156–160,
    162–165, 203, 217
as a science, 10, 11, 24–25,
    151
self-interest and, 166
short-term planning and,
    44, 45

management (*continued*)
  staffing and, 41, 44–47
  of teams, 22, 59, 200, 206,
    212–213, 214
  total quality programs and,
    200, 204–205, 207–209
  training, 3, 26–27, 65, 151
management information sys-
    tem (MIS), 7, 9
management professionals,
    200–201
Managerial Behavior (Sayles),
    28
managerial culture, 63, 65
managerial mystique, 64, 84, 86
managers. *See also* CEOs; exec-
    utives; leadership; man-
    agement
  as *bricoleurs,* 210
  conceptions of work and,
    67–69, 70
  courage and, 150, 152
  decisional roles of, 18–21, 22
  defining moments and,
    90–112
  ethical decisions and,
    90–112
  integrated roles of, 21–22
  interpersonal roles of, 13–15,
    16, 22, 71–74, 150–169
  job of, 2–32, 149–150, 203
  as monitors, 17
  obligations of, 25–26
  pace of work and, 4–6, 11, 24
  as problem solvers, 41,
    47–50, 63–64
  procedures of, 11–12

recruiting and, 138
self-study questions for,
    32–34
sense of self and, 75–76
Managers and Their Jobs (Carl-
    son), 28
marketing, 49, 132, 213–214,
    215–216
Marshall, Colin, 136–137,
    176–178
MasterCard, 53, 54
McNeil, Kathryn (pseudonym),
    99–104, 111
Mead, Dana, 140, 141, 144–145
mediocrity, causes of, 78, 149
Midway Airlines, 129
MIS. *See* management informa-
    tion system
Moments of Truth (Carlzon),
    185
monitoring role of manager, 17
Monsanto, 82
motivation, 41, 58–60, 165–166
Motorola, 130, 131, 211–212

NatWest Group (British bank),
    136
negotiator, manager as, 21
networks, 49–50
Neustadt, Richard, 9, 16, 28
New York Times, The, 109
Nicoli, Eric, 128–129
Nicolosi, Richard, 58–60
Nietzsche, Friedrich, 112

Ogilvy & Mather (advertising
    agency), 130, 132

"once-born" personality type, 75, 77
order, conceptions of, 87
organizational culture, 63, 65
organizational structure
  of Philips N.V., 81
  of Proctor & Gamble, 59
organizations
  adaptive work and, 173–197
  diversity in, 181, 182
  inertia and, 63
  influencing behavior and, 101
  information and, 183–184
  interdependence and, 44–45
  leadership development and, 80–83
  as machines, 218
  role of CEOs in, 117, 142–143
  social roles of, 107–108
  strategy and, 85–86
  strength of, 105–107
  virtual, 194
  vision and, 48
  work avoidance in, 182–183
organizing, and management, 2, 41, 44–47
originality, 152
Orr, Bobby, 175
orthodoxy, and control systems, 134

Peace, William, 156–158, 167–169
peer training, 80–81
Pennsylvania Railroad, 80

PepsiCo, 127
personality
  leadership as function of, 143–144, 145, 146
  "once-" versus "twice-born" personality types, 75, 77
Personnel (Guest), 28
Peters, Tom, 32
Philips N.V. (Dutch corporation), 81
planning, 2, 4–6
  management and, 41, 42–44, 47
  "planning dilemma" and, 24–25
"playing to win," 103–104
Polaroid, 66
power ethic, 62, 63
pragmatism
  context and, 206–209
  defined, 218
  making do and, 209–212
  management and, 203, 204–217
  19th century, 206
  outcomes and, 212–214
  uncertainty and, 214–216
predictability, and control systems, 135
Presidential Power (Neustadt), 28
Pritchard, Jack, 172–173
proactive management, 214
problem solving
  adaptive work and, 174, 184
  management and, 41, 47–50

Proctor & Gamble, 58–60, 82,
154
productivity, at Semco, 159
profit sharing, 159, 160, 163
protection, and adaptive work,
180
Pump, The (Reebok product),
215–216

quality
quality circles and,
207–208
quality control and, 160
total quality management
and, 200, 204–205, 207,
209

race, and defining moments,
93–98, 111
R&D, 49, 128, 138–139
recruitment, 138
Reebok, 215–216
reengineering, 208, 218
regulation, 133, 144
Rely tampon crisis, 154
renewal, 138
resource allocation, 20–21
responsibility
adaptive work and, 174,
183–185
collective, 177
employees and, 184
management and, 156–158,
159–160, 162–165, 203,
217
Reuter, Edzard, 121–122

risk-taking
adaptive work and, 194
among CEOs, 126, 137
among employees, 55, 138
Rockefeller, John D., III, 63
Roosevelt, Franklin Delano, 9,
16, 28
Rosenberg, Richard, 136, 144
Rosenbluth, Hal, 152–154
Rosenbluth, Marcus, 152–154
Rosenbluth Travel, 152–154
Roussel Uclaf (French com-
pany), 106–111
RU-486 (drug), 106–111, 112

safety, and control systems,
133
Sakiz, Eduoard, 106–112
SAS. *See* Scandinavian Airlines
Systems
Sayer Microworld, 99–104,
111
Sayles, Leonard R., 19, 28
Scandinavian Airlines Systems
(SAS), 43, 182, 184–185
Scott, Thomas A., 80
*Second American Revolution,
The* (Rockefeller), 63
self-confidence, 185
self-deception, 155
self-interest, 166
Sells, Bill, 154–156
Semco, 158–160
Semler, Ricardo, 158–160
short-term planning, 44, 45
shrewdness, 96–98

Sloan, Alfred P., 67–69
Southwest Airlines, 127–128, 129, 145
spokesperson, manager's role as, 17
sports, and leadership, 175
staffing, 41, 44–47
Stayer, Ralph, 160–161, 162
Stewart, Rosemary, 14–15
stockholders, and vision, 43
strategic alliances, 194
strategy
approach to leadership, 118–119, 122–126, 137
creativity and, 191–192
importance of, 85–86
at KPMG Netherlands, 187–194
Street Corner Society (Whyte), 29
Synthetic Fuels Division (Westinghouse), 156–158, 167–169

teams. *See also* work groups
cross-functional, 173, 220
management of, 22, 59, 200, 206, 212–213, 214
Tenneco, 140, 144–145
Thompson, Julian Ogilvie, 130, 132
3M, 51–52
total quality management (TQM), 200, 204–205, 207, 209

training
management, 3, 26–27, 65, 151
peer, 80–81
travel, 126–127, 153–154
Travel Related Services (American Express), 53–55
trouble-makers, 141
Trowbridge, Chuck, 56–58
TRS, 53–55
Truman, Harry S., 9, 28
trust
British Airways and, 177
communication and, 49
"twice-born" personality type, 75, 77

United Biscuits (British company), 128

values
at British Airways, 177
"company way" and, 129
core, 91–92, 95–96, 108
family-oriented, 99–104
Varieties of Religious Experience, The (James), 75
virtual organizations, 194
Visa, 53, 54
vision. *See also* goals
CEOs and, 122
customers and, 43
development of, 41
effectiveness and, 42–43
employees and, 43, 48
energy and, 48

vision (*continued*)
  as hallmark of leadership, 86
  organizations and, 48
  stockholders and, 43
  "voices from below," 185–187

Wanless, Derek, 136
Waterman, Robert, 32
Welch, Jack, 207–208
Westinghouse, 156–158,
  167–169
Whyte, William F., 29
work. *See also* adaptive work
  avoidance of, 182–183
  conceptions of, 67–70

work groups, 98–104. *See also*
  teams
working mothers, 99–104
Work-Out program (General
  Electric), 207–208
World War II, and pragmatic
  action, 217
W.R. Grace, 140

Zaleznik, Abraham, 28–29
Zeien, Al, 127, 128